D1526511

MODERN
NATIONS
—OF THE—
WORLD

NORWAY

TITLES IN THE MODERN NATIONS OF THE WORLD SERIES INCLUDE:

Austria
Brazil
Canada
China
Cuba
Egypt
England
Ethiopia
Germany
Greece
Haiti
India
Ireland
Italy
Japan
Jordan
Kenya
Mexico
Poland
Russia
Saudi Arabia
Scotland
Somalia
South Africa
South Korea
Spain
Sweden
Switzerland
Taiwan
The United States
Vietnam

MODERN
NATIONS
—OF THE—
WORLD

NORWAY

BY LAUREL CORONA

LUCENT BOOKS
P.O. BOX 289011
SAN DIEGO, CA 92198-9011

On Cover: Alesund, Norway.

To Elisabeth Willanger, with thanks for her help in researching this book.

Library of Congress Cataloging-in-Publication Data

Corona, Laurel, 1949–
  Norway / by Laurel Corona.
     p. cm. — (Modern nations of the world)
  Includes bibliographical references and index.
  Summary: Discusses Norway including its history, people, arts and enter-
  tainment, and future.
   ISBN 1-56006-647-4 (alk. paper)
   1.Norway—Juvenile literature. I. Title. II. Series.
   DL409.C66 2001
   948. 1—dc21
                                                       00-010263

Copyright © 2001 by Lucent Books, Inc.
P.O. Box 289011, San Diego, CA 92198-9011
Printed in the U.S.A.

CONTENTS

INTRODUCTION   6
Islands, Tunnels, and Bridges

CHAPTER ONE   13
A Rugged Land and People

CHAPTER TWO   30
The Land of the Vikings

CHAPTER THREE   44
A Country Lost and Regained

CHAPTER FOUR   60
Norwegians at Work and Play

CHAPTER FIVE   77
Arts and Entertainment

CHAPTER SIX   92
Facing the Future

Facts About Norway   105
Notes   108
Chronology   111
Glossary   114
Suggestions for Further Reading   116
Works Consulted   118
Index   120
Picture Credits   127
About the Author   128

INTRODUCTION
ISLANDS, TUNNELS, AND BRIDGES

For most of its length, a narrow strip of thousands of islands scattered along the coast of the Norwegian and Barents Seas guards the Norway coast. The coastline itself is a jumble of bays and inlets called fjords, most of them surrounded by jagged mountain peaks. So convoluted is this coastline that if it were pulled out into a straight line it would stretch halfway around the world. For thousands of years travel in many parts of Norway was only possible by use of small boats along the coast in summer, or by skis on land in winter. Even today in parts of the country skis and boats are still the easiest ways to get around. Because of the difficulty of travel and a relatively small amount of land suited for agriculture, much of Norway consists of small villages and farms sprinkled along the coast and in the inland valleys and mountains. It is no wonder, then, that Norway, with 4.4 million people, is the least densely populated country in Europe although the fifth largest in terms of land.

The challenge of keeping Norwegians connected with each other is best illustrated by looking at a map. Norway's northeastern border with Russia is almost as far east as Istanbul, Turkey. If the city of Kristiansand, located on the south coast, were used as the axis and the entire country were rotated south, the normally northernmost town of Hammerfest would now be as far south as Rome. The famed Hurtigruten coastal steamer takes eleven days to travel the round trip between Bergen and Kirkenes, and its route does not even cover the southern end of the country. Yet despite the great distances between one region and another, Norwegians have a strong national identity and sense of unity.

FROM VIKINGS TO VIDKUN QUISLING

This national unity and identity has been hard won. Typically when people think of Norway's past, they first think of the Vikings, whose raids along the European coast and deep into the Mediterranean—and whose discovery of the New World—changed the course of history. Although no outsider challenged Viking power in Norway and few could successfully stand in their way when they ventured abroad, the Viking era nevertheless ended nearly a millennium ago. In the past six hundred years, the story has been quite different. Beginning with a political alliance between Scandinavian royalty in 1397 A.D., Norway saw its prior independent status gradually erode to the point where it was treated simply as a province of Denmark. Early in the nineteenth century Norway became aligned with Sweden, and though Norway was supposedly independent and coequal, the truth was far from that. Desire for independence grew over the course of the century and was finally achieved in 1905.

After Norway achieved independence, however, it continued to struggle to remain free of foreign rule. Early in World

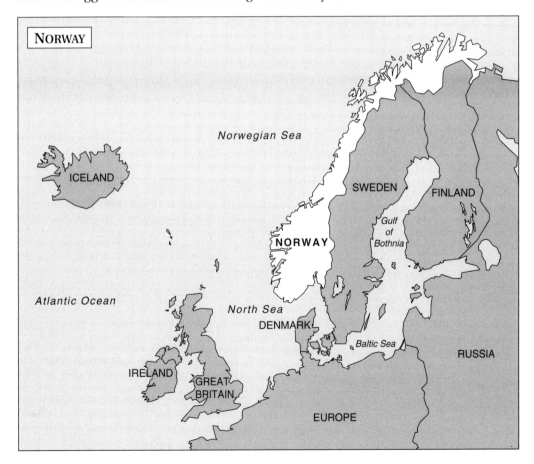

War II, the German army invaded and set up a "puppet government," with Norwegians sympathetic to the Nazi cause in charge. One such Norwegian was Vidkun Quisling, to whom Hitler gave the special title of Minister President. As a result, the world gained a new word, "quisling," still used today to mean a traitor. Norwegian resistance to the Nazis is legendary, but in retaliation, the Nazis in their retreat left few of the towns of coastal Norway standing. After the war, Norway remained vigilant along its northeast border with the Soviet Union, fearful that the region's mineral riches might give the Soviets ideas about adding Norway to their empire. Today, since the fall of the Soviet Union, no one threatens Norway's borders. In fact, Norway has become a powerful and respected part of the international community for its peacekeeping efforts elsewhere in the world.

A NETWORK OF ISLANDS

Out of their struggles, the Norwegian people have bonded into a strong nation. Yet the facts of geography remain, and the Norwegian character has been shaped over the centuries by a population typically isolated in small valleys, on little islands, or along remote fjords, as well as by the need to overcome this solitude.

In Norway one cannot travel far without coming to water or mountains that must be crossed, and such barriers are where Norwegian commitment to national unity is most clearly tested. Even in the most lightly populated areas, roads disappear into tunnels that run under stretches of deep, green water, trains roar into openings blasted into the sides of rocky cliffs, and graceful bridges span fjords and ocean channels. Clearly, Norway has met and will continue to meet the challenge of keeping its people connected.

Whereas in some other countries, many small towns have been abandoned and people have flocked to cities, Norwegians are committed to keeping their small-town culture alive. Their network of tunnels and bridges is one way Norwegians bring the benefits of the modern world to rural areas, allowing local residents to stay where they are. Today, when teenagers graduate from a rural high school, they can even go to a university in one of the small nearby cities if they wish, and so remain closely linked to their home communities. The government also supports farmers, who might not

be able to make ends meet on their small plots of land, by paying subsidies and stipends to keep them raising their livestock and planting their fields. These programs cost money, and Norwegians are heavily taxed to maintain strong rural communities. But the result has been a culture more helped than damaged by modernization and progress.

The Norwegian landscape features many mountains and bodies of water, forcing Norwegians to form small, independent communities.

PUBLIC AND PRIVATE LIFE

Thus, the typical Norwegian has both a regional and a national identity—sometimes balancing two distinct forms of the Norwegian language, *bokmål* and *nynorsk,* to reflect this split. But Norwegians are also very individualistic. They treasure their time away from crowds, even if the crowd is only a few other people in the local market, and their personal lives focus on family and close friends. Norwegians understand and respect each other's need to spend time alone, preferably outdoors, on a ski trail or walking through the woods. Even in a crowded city, most Norwegians keep to themselves, avoiding eye contact and conversation on buses, and disappearing quickly for home as soon as the work day is over. Perhaps the best illustration of this understood need for privacy is a law that states it is permissible to camp anywhere in Norway for one night, as long as one stays 150 meters away from the nearest dwelling. Even on their private, occupied land, owners do not object to such overnight visits, because they understand the camper's need to be in the open air, and the owners are likely to have taken advantage of the law themselves. As long as the landowner's privacy is respected, the passing visitor is welcome.

Perhaps due to the isolated nature of their communities, Norwegians tend to avoid crowds and take pleasure in open spaces.

Each Norwegian is indeed like a little island. Perhaps this temperament evolved through centuries of isolation on rural farms, where in months of winter darkness families huddled around the wood stove, comfortable in their long silences. Little happened that required much discussion, and people living in such quarters learned it was best to avoid the antagonisms that words can spark. Sociologists often remark that in cultures where people must live very closely together, customs such as not looking directly at one another or not speaking to strangers evolve to maintain a sense of privacy. Even far away from snow-covered farms in modern cities like Oslo, such old habits linger.

Yet the image of Norway populated by 4.4 million individual "islands" is deceptive. Just as a Norwegian island may look isolated but have a high tech underwater tunnel connecting it to some other place, Norwegians themselves have strong links to each other. And although their individual families, and particularly the children in them, are clearly the center of most lives, Norwegians are extraordinarily socially conscious and generally supportive of governmental and other efforts to provide a good quality of life for everyone around them. Even though urban Norwegians may not stop to chat with their neighbors on street corners, they do care that those neighbors have medical care when ill, an adequate pension when retired, and good schools to which to send their children.

In recent decades, however, taxes have not covered the cost of most government services and programs. Although the tax rate is high by European standards, it is actually the profits from oil and natural gas fields off the Norwegian coast that have been keeping many social programs afloat. Concerns have grown that in the future, as income from these natural resources shrinks, Norwegians' generosity of spirit toward their fellow citizens may be severely tested.

THE JANTE LAW

Part of the Norwegian concern with a decent standard of living for all is reflected in what is known as the Jante Law, from a fictional character created by writer Aksel Sandemose. Not an official law, but simply an expression of a way of thinking, the Jante Law states in essence that no one should ever think that he or she is better than anyone else. Norwegians feel that it is good to be neither too poor nor too rich—nor stand out in any way—and that the goal of government, and of society as a whole, should be to level the playing field for all. Sociologists often attribute this attitude to the difficulty of life in a hostile climate, and the consequent need for everyone to contribute to the survival of others. Even the royal family of Norway takes pains to present itself as normal in every way, and their payoff has been the continued affection of the Norwegian people for the monarchy. The current king, Harald V, was once asked why he often went out without a bodyguard. His reply was that he had over four million of them.

Although many feel that the idea behind the Jante Law is a good and valid one, others point to some negative consequences. Overall, brilliance in any area is not encouraged because it sets individuals apart, encouraging some to consider themselves better than others. In school, the brightest students are not encouraged to move through the curriculum

Norway relies heavily upon income from oil and natural gas fields to fund its social programs.

more quickly and are not given additional work to do because many Norwegians feel that the greater good is served by not having such students see themselves as intellectually superior. Though there is a kindness to the slower pupils at the core of it, this philosophy does not produce many great artists or visionary leaders.

Visionaries will be needed as Norway moves into the future. The country faces new challenges to its national identity as more and more immigrants see the benefits of moving to this peaceful, socially advanced country. Norway cherishes its role in international diplomacy and is likely to continue to be needed in that capacity around the world. It will have to find a way to maintain social services and its standard of living in the face of falling oil and natural gas revenues and the challenges of immigration. Norway will need to manage its waters and forests well so as not to endanger further its fish, mammals, and plants. It will need to continue to develop transportation and other linkages among its remote communities. But few doubt that Norway will come out well in the years to come because the country has such a strong base on which to build, and a strong desire to remain a vital nation.

A RUGGED LAND AND PEOPLE

If Norway were to be captured in a single image it would be as a house, brightly painted blue or red, green or yellow, with contrasting trim around the windows and doors, all topped by a pointed roof. This house would be sitting alone, or perhaps in a small cluster of homes, against a backdrop of awesome natural majesty. The setting might be on sea cliffs

For Norwegians, the central focus of life lies in their homes and the rugged landscape surrounding them. 13

rising nearly straight up from a narrow coastal valley. It might be below jagged mountain peaks, still snow-covered in July, pushing relentlessly upward from an inland valley. Or it might be on a low-lying island surrounded by crashing seas and defended only by the lonely beam of a lighthouse tower. All of these are equally typical images, for they combine the two most essential elements of Norwegian existence—home and rugged nature.

In fact, one of the most surprising things about Norway is how few scenes, regardless of how remote, lack some sign of human habitation. High above the cliffs surrounding such fjords as the Geiranger hang little mountain meadows with farmhouses and barns, accessible only by a narrow footpath from the water below. Even in the bitter darkness of an Arc-

STAVE CHURCHES

Scattered across Norway, particularly in the central regions, are the thirty-two surviving stave churches which typify the traditional architecture of Norway. To build a stave church a series of poles was set in the ground, and at certain heights a wooden ring was formed connecting these poles. Long strips of timber were slotted into the rings to form the walls of the church. Amazingly, very elaborate structures with towers and many roof sections, as well as wings jutting out from the main floor space, could be made by this stave technique—all without a single nail. The entire stave church is held together by the slotted boards.

The stave churches have dragon heads jutting out from their roofs, evoking the prow of Viking ships. The church doors and portals are also richly carved with mythological symbols. The roofs and outer walls are usually covered with decorative and contrasting wood designs, making the overall effect one of many tiny and repeated patterns. The church interiors are always extremely dark, because windows were not—for reasons of weather and building style—part of the overall design. But there was always a small opening from the outside, through which lepers could listen to the service.

About 750 stave churches were built, most from 1150 A.D. to 1250 A.D., making the 29 which survive in Norway today among the world's oldest wooden buildings. Most of the other stave churches were torn down during the religious frenzy of the Pietists in the eighteenth century, who saw the work of the devil in these old, graceful treasures from another time.

tic winter, each valley seems to have at least one smoking chimney and welcoming light. Whether they dwell along the water, in one of the beautiful inland valleys, on one of the mountaintops of the interior along Norway's long border with Sweden, or in bustling downtown Oslo, Norwegians seem capable of living—and thriving—anywhere.

FJORDS AND ISLANDS

Many Norwegians inhabit a coastline fringed with countless numbers of fjords and islands. Fjords can resemble huge bays stretching for many miles, such as the Oslofjord or the Trondheimfjord, on which are situated two of the major cities of Norway, Oslo and Trondheim. Fjords can be narrow and short, such as the picturesque Trollfjord, only about a mile long and three hundred feet wide, flanked by sheer cliffs from which waterfalls tumble to emerald green water. The fjords were formed during previous ice ages, when the entire country of Norway was covered with glaciers, huge rivers of ice. The glaciers tore through the earth as they moved, scouring out long indentations in the rock. As the planet later warmed and these glaciers retreated, the indentations flooded with seawater, forming fjords.

The fjords are one of the two characteristic elements of the geography of the Norwegian coast. The other element is the thousands of islands lining that coast, making an effective barrier to the rough waters of the Norwegian Sea to the west and the Barents Sea to the north. Some of these islands, most notably the Vesterålen and the Lofoten Islands, are fairly large. Others are small, covering only a few acres, and tend to have one of two characteristic shapes. They either are low, covered with moss or grass, or else they jut out dramatically from the ocean, their gray spires providing nesting grounds for thousands of birds.

Dotted about on many of these islands are isolated cottages used in the past as temporary shelters by fishermen away from home. By use of such shelters, fishermen could avoid having to live continuously at sea. Today, many of these fishermen's cottages have been refurbished with kitchens and indoor plumbing to serve as short-term vacation rentals. People bring their small boats and their cars and settle in, having no more pressing business than spending the day trying to catch something for dinner.

NORWAY'S ISLANDS AND FJORDS

Arctic
Ocean

Porsangen Fjord   Lakse Fjord
North Cape   Tana Fjord
Hammerfest
Kirkenes

Tromso

VESTERALEN
ISLANDS

LOFOTEN
ISLANDS
Vest   Narvik
Fjord

Bodo

Norwegian
Sea   NORWAY

FINLAND

Namsen River

Trondheimfjord

Kristiansund
Trondheim
Ålesund
Geiranger Fjord   Molde   Roros
DOVRE
MOUNTAINS
Galdhöpiggen ▲   SWEDEN   Gulf
Sogne Fjord   ▲ Glittertind   of
Jostedals Glacier ▲   Bothnia
Lillehammer
JOTUNHEIMEN
Bergen
Folgefonn
Hardanger Fjord   Oslo ★
Bokn Fjord
Stavanger   Baltic   ESTONIA
Gløma River   Sea
Otra River
Oslofjord
North Sea   Kristiansand

COASTAL COMMUNITIES

There are hundreds of permanent, year-round communities
around the fjords and on the islands as well. Some have only
a few dozen residents, but others have many thousands. In
fact, all the major cities of Norway are located on a fjord. Most
common in the fjord region are communities of a few hundred to a few thousand residents. Typically these communi-

ties consist of a small town center, with one or more business streets. There may or may not be a central town square, but if there is, it is likely to be graced by a statue—often contemporary and of high artistic merit—depicting some aspect of fishing life. The statue may be of a woman in wind-whipped clothing looking anxiously out to sea for her husband and sons; or of a single fisherman in a small boat harpooning a whale; or perhaps of a famous Norwegian maritime figure, such as noted polar explorer Roald Amundsen.

Life in the town itself centers around the harbor and the docks. All day, boats bring and take away individuals doing business in the town. Every day of the year in three dozen communities between Bergen in the south and Kirkenes in the north, one or another of the eleven Hurtigruten coastal steamers stops to load and unload cargo and to discharge its load of tourists, who then may spend an hour or so racing through the town in search of souvenirs or perhaps just taking a slow walk on dry land. The coastal steamer is also a vital link for residents, who use it to go between towns not easily reached by roads, often driving their cars on board at one port and driving off again at a different port a little further along the route.

One of the major cities in Norway, Stavanger, is home to the Stavanger cathedral, on which work began in 1125.

The highest building in town is usually the church, a tall steeple rising up from a typically box-shaped building. Few of these churches are genuinely old, however, especially in the north. At the end of World War II, the retreating German army reduced nearly every community to rubble and ash and forced the evacuation of residents. But communities were quickly rebuilt after the war, and while some ports are now an unappealing jumble of ugly buildings in poor repair, most communities contain the classic symbols of Norwegian life—the steepled church and rows of brightly colored homes.

STAVANGER

The coast of Norway can be divided into three sections, the southern and northern ends of the country, with a long stretch of fjords and islands in between. Three of the major cities of Norway—Stavanger, Bergen and Trondheim—are located in this middle region. Stavanger has approximately one hundred thousand residents,

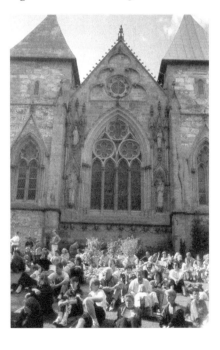

most making a living through shipping or fishing. Stavanger has a long history, dating from the Battle of Hafrsfjord in 872 A.D., just outside today's city, where Viking chieftain Harold Hårfagri's victory united the country. Work on the Stavanger cathedral began in 1125, and since medieval times the city has grown and prospered, in large measure due to the richness of Norwegian fisheries. According to author Robert Spark, in the first half of the twentieth century there were over seventy canneries employing three quarters of the population, and, "the smell of oily fish hung over the town, permeating every breath. But Stavanger was never in doubt about the value of that smell, [saying] 'don't scorn it, that's the smell of money.'"[1]

Stavanger was best known to Americans in the nineteenth and early twentieth centuries as the port of embarkation for Norwegian emigrants to the United States. Today the city attracts many of these emigrants' descendants back as tourists, who then often flock to historic Old Stavanger, a district still lit by old fashioned street lamps and paved in cobblestones. Beyond the historic district, modern prosperity (largely a result of the discovery of oil in the Norwegian Sea) is apparent in the city's many factories and businesses.

LEMMINGS

Lemmings are common Norwegian rodents with an uncommon life pattern. Every eleven or twelve years, the lemming population grows so suddenly and massively that in former times the Vikings believed lemmings fell from the sky during thunderstorms.

According to Jules Brown and Phil Lee, writing in *Norway: The Rough Guide,* "in these so called 'lemming years,' the mountains and surrounding areas teem with countless thousands of lemmings and hundreds swarm to their deaths by falling off cliff edges and the like." Though most humans find the swarming lemmings repulsive, predators for whom the yellowish, squeaking lemmings are a food source have a wonderful time during lemming years, often doubling their own number of young. In one of the great mysteries of animal behavior, the snowy owl, which does not share the same habitat as the lemmings, leaves its polar region only in lemming years to fly down to the area where the lemmings live. What triggers the owl's knowledge that a particular year is a lemming year is completely unknown.

BERGEN

Bergen, with 213,000 inhabitants, is the second largest city in Norway after the capital, Oslo. Situated at the southern end of central Norway, Bergen is a major shipping port, as well as a cultural and tourist center. Bergen is known for its scenic setting and also for its rainy weather, typical of the west coast of Norway. A common joke about the city concerns a visitor to Bergen who asks a boy if it always rains there. The boy replies that he doesn't know because he's only twelve.

Rain or shine, the historic heart of Bergen is the harbor. There in the market, or *torget*, merchant stalls line the harborside square, displaying the day's catch. Nestled against one of Bergen's seven hills is the Bryggen, a wharf area dating back many centuries; the Bryggen consists of a warren of small streets lined with wooden shops and houses. Tourists must dodge artisans and fishermen along the alleyways, because the Bryggen is still very much a working community. Also in the Bryggen is the entrance to the Fløibanen, a cable car which climbs one thousand feet above Bergen. At the top, visitors can walk along forest paths and enjoy the spectacular view.

The second largest city in Norway, Bergen, is a major shipping port, in addition to being a cultural and tourist center.

Bergen is also well known among lovers of the arts. Its symphony orchestra is among the oldest in the world, and the Bergen International Music Festival in May is one of the most prestigious events of its kind. Just outside the city are the historic homes of composer Edvard Grieg and violinist Ole Bull, the homes now museums and concert sites. Also in Bergen are a major university and a world-famous aquarium.

TRONDHEIM

Trondheim is the third largest city in Norway, with 140,000 inhabitants. It is located about a third of the way up the coast on a massive fjord which stretches halfway across the country toward the Swedish border. Trondheim is situated right where Norway's bulbous southern tip narrows to the thin coastal strip which characterizes the rest of the country's length to the north.

The capital of Norway in the Viking era, Trondheim is the third largest city in Norway. The river Nid runs through Trondheim, and is lined by eighteenth-century warehouses, now used as shops and restaurants.

Trondheim, formerly called Nidaros, was the capital of Norway in the Viking era. It was a logical choice for a center owing to its well-protected port and its location at the edge of a large, fertile valley. The remarkable Nidaros cathedral, the largest medieval church in Scandinavia, still looms above the skyline. Olav Haraldsson, a Viking king, was killed in a battle at nearby Stiklestad in 1030 A.D., and buried in what was then the small town of Trondheim. Rumors abounded that his body had not rotted after death, and he was soon canonized as Saint Olav. The cathedral was built to honor him, and Trondheim became a major pilgrimage site as well as an important port. For many years it was the main city in Norway, although it has now been eclipsed by Oslo and Bergen. Still, coronations of the Swedish king take place in Nidaros cathedral, in deference to its unique role, not just in Norway's history but in that of Scandinavia as a whole.

A river, the Nid (Nidaros means mouth of the Nid), runs through Trondheim, and many of the city's sights lie along or close to its banks. Old eighteenth-century warehouses, many now converted to shops and restaurants, line the river and the harbor, their bright colors reflected in the calm waters of the Nid. Trondheim also is home to one of the major universities in Norway, as well as to several important museums.

THE SAMI

The northernmost parts of Norway, Sweden, and Finland—along with the Kola Peninsula of Russia—form a region called Lapland. Lapland is home to an ethnically distinct group of people formerly called Lapps, but now called by their preferred name, the Sami. There are approximately seventy thousand Sami today, the majority of whom live in Norway. They are known for their colorful red costumes and their brightly colored four-cornered hats, as well as for a unique style of song called a *yoik*. Many people first learned of the Sami while watching the opening ceremony of the Lillehammer Winter Olympic Games in 1994, when forty reindeer pulling traditional Sami sleds dashed into the stadium along with their owners.

Ethnically unrelated to Norwegians, the Sami speak a language related to Finnish and Hungarian, evidence that many centuries ago this region as well as Finland must have been populated by a group which came north from the area of modern Hungary, in central Europe. The Sami kept apart from other Scandinavian cultures for centuries, focusing on their own main activity, reindeer herding, as well as on farming and fishing. In recent years, however, as more and more people have come to northernmost Norway because of tourism, oil field development, and other reasons, many Sami have stopped living in their traditional ways and now dwell in towns and work at regular jobs.

After the Russian nuclear disaster at Chernobyl in 1986, the Sami reindeer herds were damaged by radioactive fallout, which poisoned the lichens and moss on which the reindeer feed. This disaster to their herds was a blow to the Sami, but was not the first such blow they have had to weather. For centuries efforts to "Norwegianize" the Sami forced them to convert to Christianity, go to Norwegian schools, and use Norwegian as their language. In the last few decades, however, the government has reversed its position, and now efforts are being made to preserve the Sami culture. A new Sami parliament has been established, and although it is only advisory to the Norwegian government, the decisions and opinions of the Sami parliament are taken seriously. Courses in Sami language, literature, and history are common in colleges and universities, and younger children learn about Sami history in school. Where once the Sami were so looked down upon that many of them tried to hide their roots, now being Sami is once again a source of great pride.

Ethnically unrelated to Norwegians, the Sami are trying to preserve their culture, which centers on reindeer herding, farming, and fishing.

ARCTIC NORWAY

Trondheim lies about halfway between Bergen and the Arctic town of Bodø. Bodø, with thirty-eight thousand residents, is the first major population center inside the Arctic Circle. Further north, the days with summer's midnight sun or winter's midday darkness increase, having a major impact on life. The winter cold lingers longer in the north, and the growing season there is very short. Farmers are limited to crops like strawberries, which can grow quickly once the weather warms. Even further north, wild plant species dwindle, and all trees except for birches thin out and then disappear completely. Northwards again, even the birch can no longer survive, and plant life is limited to mosses, the favorite food of the reindeer herds that are the livelihood of the Sami, Norway's indigenous people.

Undeterred by the harsh climate, many Norwegians live inside the Arctic Circle. Part of their reason for sticking out the tough winters is the availability of work. In this region huge oil and natural gas fields have been discovered and are now being tapped. Iron ore deposits are extensive as well, and there are valuable mines of copper and other metals. But fishing is king, and from the waters off Arctic Norway comes much of the world's supply of cod as well as several other commercially valuable fish species.

In addition to Bodø, there are the sizable towns of Narvik and Tromsø. Narvik, according to writers Jules Brown and Phil Lee, "makes no bones about its main function: the iron ore

Norwegians relax on a summer afternoon in Tromsø, an old town dating from the thirteenth century.

docks are immediately conspicuous, slap bang in the centre of town . . . overwhelming the whole waterfront."[2] The town was established by workers building the railroad between mines and the docks. It was totally leveled at the end of World War II, and has been rebuilt without even a nod to charm. Still, Narvik provides steady employment for its residents.

Tromsø is a very old town, dating from the thirteenth century. With a population of fifty thousand, it has a university (the world's northernmost) and two large churches, in Norway called cathedrals. The Arctic Cathedral is a relatively new landmark, completed in 1965. Its steep white roof resembles a glacier and the entire east wall is a massive, modern stained-glass window, one of the largest in Europe. The other cathedral is a traditional wooden structure, located in the middle of town, whose grounds provide a meeting place for the local population. The town also has a busy harbor and a shopping district.

Even further north lies Hammerfest—the northernmost town in the world—and Kirkenes, a rugged outpost on the Russian border. Hammerfest, remarkably, was the first European town to have its streets lit by electricity, owing to the far-sightedness of a local leader who saw the advantages of having good lights in the Arctic winter. Hammerfest is a prosperous town, with a fish processing plant that is the main employer of its seven thousand residents. Kirkenes, with six thousand inhabitants, is a center for fishing and forestry, also for mining and the shipping of iron ore. According to author Robert Spark,

> the town's somewhat rough and ready appearance is explained and easily forgiven when you learn that the 20th century has brought no less than four wars fought in or near it. World War II brought the most suffering when, apart from Malta [in the Mediterranean], Kirkenes acquired the unsolicited honour of being the most bombed centre in Europe.[3]

ARCTIC SIGHTS

Natural landmarks of the Arctic region include the Vesterålen and Lofoten Islands, where vegetation, especially in areas unprotected from the wind, is mostly thick layers of moss. Orcas, or killer whales, often swim in the straits between these islands. A more common sight between March and June is that of huge drying racks in fishing villages, where hundreds of

THE SKIES OVER NORWAY

Northern Norway is inside the Arctic Circle, and this location subjects it to two of the world's most interesting natural phenomena. The first of these is the midnight sun, a result of the changing angle of the earth's axis as it circles the sun. At midnight the sun drops to just above the horizon before rising again, but never leaves the sky. In Bodø, a city near the edge of the Arctic Circle, the midnight sun appears only for a few weeks, from early June to mid-July, but farther north, in the town of Hammerfest, the northernmost city in Norway, the midnight sun shines from mid-May to the end of July.

Six months later, the Arctic Circle is plunged into darkness for months at a time. In Bodø only faint glimmers of what looks like dawn light the sky for a few hours in December. Farther north the darkness is more total and lasts longer. In Hammerfest, for example, after the sun sets on November 20, it will not be seen again until January 23.

However, from time to time, when atmospheric conditions are right, the darkness provides a splendor of its own—the second important phenomenon. The northern lights, or *aurora borealis,* are a spectacular natural light show which fills the winter sky with patterns of usually green—but occasionally yellow, red, or violet—lights which swirl and dance, sometimes for hours. The lights are caused by charged particles sent out from the sun in what is called the solar wind. These particles are pulled into the earth's magnetic field and collide with matter in the earth's atmosphere, releasing light. The earth's magnetic field in the polar region causes the lights to appear as long tails or ribbons across the sky. The lights appear only from time to time because the conditions under which these colliding particles will create light are fairly specific, but for lucky visitors to the Arctic Circle, the experience is one they will remember forever.

thousands of cod, called *klippfisk,* hang until they are hard as boards and ready for export.

Perhaps the most famous Arctic landmark is the North Cape, or Nordkapp in Norwegian. Located in Finnmark, the northernmost region of Norway, the North Cape is often erroneously celebrated as the northernmost point in Europe. In fact that distinction should go to Knivskjellodden, one promontory over. However, North Cape, so named by British explorer Richard

Chancellor in 1533, is the traditional place to go if one wishes to stand on the most remote edge of Europe. Seventeenth-century explorer Francesco Negri exclaimed when he visited, "where the world comes to an end, my curiosity does as well, and now I can return home content."[4]

SOUTHERN NORWAY

The southern end of Norway provides a stark visual contrast to the Arctic north, but in fact has many similarities to it. Except for the nation's capital, Oslo, and a few cities along the southern coast, the entire bulbous region of south Norway is also characterized by small communities as in the north. However, unlike the north, the south is a rich agricultural area. The south also contains colorful and scenic mountains and lush valleys.

The Telemark region in southern Norway is fabled as the birthplace of skiing. Mountainous and isolated, Telemark has retained much of its old-world customs and charm. According to Robert Spark, "throughout Telemark one senses an older Norway lurking just beneath the surface. The upper districts were, until recently, impenetrable except on skis, travel in winter being easier than in summer."[5] Telemark still has today at Heddal some of the finest old buildings, such as the twelfth-century stave church (so called because it is constructed of slotted upright boards, or staves). Telemark also has the best preserved folk art traditions, such as the type of wood painting called *rosemaling,* to be found anywhere in Norway.

Located in southern Norway, the Telemark region lends its name to a graceful form of downhill skiing.

THE HARDANGER PLATEAU AND JOTUNHEIMEN

North of Telemark, and lying between Oslo and Bergen, is the huge Hardangervidda, or Hardanger plateau. North of the plateau lies the "Home of the Giants," or Jotunheimen. According to writer Robert Spark, in these two areas "centres of population are few, places of interest are also thin on the ground, but of superb scenery—mountains, glaciers, lakes, and rivers—there is an excess."[6]

In fact, what attracts people to the Hardangervidda is its isolation. The center of the plateau has many lakes, streams, and waterfalls, as well as three main valleys—the Begnadalen, Hallingdalen, and Numendalen. At higher altitudes, the climate is like the Arctic, so much so that reindeer are a common sight. The Oslo–Bergen railroad line, which cuts across the Hardangervidda, creates one of the most beautiful rail journeys in the world.

THE GULF STREAM

The southernmost point in Norway is further north than the northern tip of Scotland, and Norway actually lies in the same latitude as Greenland. Human habitation in much of Norway, and year-round travel among its harbors, is possible only because of the Gulf Stream.

The Gulf Stream is a current of relatively warm water which flows across the Atlantic from the Gulf of Mexico. The Gulf Stream is approximately sixty miles wide and moves 25 million cubic meters of water every second. It passes around the British Isles, and then continues north up the Norwegian coast, keeping the water along that coast too warm to freeze. Thus, although lakes and some shallow ocean waters freeze solid enough to walk on, the deep fjords and the coastal waters do not, and shipping lanes can remain open all year. The Gulf Stream does not reach the Barents Sea, which reaches across the top of Scandinavia. Ports there, including the Norwegian town of Kirkenes, often must break up ice in their harbors.

As a side effect of its warmer water, the Gulf Stream also keeps the air temperature in coastal Norway higher than it otherwise would be. Although winters are still very cold, coastal dwellers do not experience the extreme bitter cold of equally northern places such as Greenland or Siberia, or even much of the rest of Scandinavia.

An open air museum in Lillehammer provides a picturesque and informative stopping point for visitors.

Jotunheimen is known as the Home of the Giants because here are found the two highest mountains in Norway, Gald-hopiggen and Glittertinden, both a little over eight thousand feet in height. In the southern part of Jotunheimen, Lake Gjende draws visitors to its green waters and high surrounding peaks. Visitors come for the scenery, but often make a stop at Borgund, to look at a stave church dating from 1150 A.D. and reputed to be the best preserved and most typical in Norway. Nearby national parks are Rondane and Dovrefjell. Both have excellent hiking trails, and provide opportunities for viewing the wildlife of the region. Many summer hikers come away complaining, however, that the most ferocious creatures they encountered were the mosquitoes!

THE HEARTLAND

Between Oslo and Trondheim is what many consider to be the true heartland of Norway. The region around Norway's largest lake, Lake Mjøsa, is one of the most fertile agricultural areas in the country. Four towns are situated on the lake, including Hamar, a small town today but once the center of the medieval Catholic church in Norway. The most important town on Lake Mjøsa, however, is Lillehammer, site of the 1994 Winter Olympics. Lillehammer is the major winter sports center for the entire country and is also known for its open-air museum, the largest in northern Europe. The museum was the dream of one man, Anders Sandvig, who was responsible for relocating approximately 140 buildings to the site. The museum includes a stave church, mountain grazing huts, and two small seventeenth-century farms, complete with all the outlying buildings and livestock grazing on the grounds.

About one hundred miles north of Lillehammer is the copper mining town of Røros. The region surrounding Røros is rich in a variety of minerals and metals, but the beauty of the scenery is occasionally marred by the scars of mining. Røros is unique in Norway in that its entire old town section must by law remain exactly as it was. However, it is not a ghost town—all the historic buildings must be lived in, although maintained in strict conformity to the look of the town three hundred years ago, including the grass-covered roofs.

OSLO

After spending time in older communities like Røros, visitors to Oslo are often surprised by how new the city is. Although many of Oslo's views are dominated by the Akershus, a castle dating from the 1300s, and although the city itself can trace roots back to the year 1000 A.D., most of what can be seen today dates from no earlier than the late nineteenth century. The hub of Oslo is the pedestrian-only thoroughfare called Karl Johan's Gate. Lined with stores, cafes, and clubs, it runs between the royal palace and the central train station and attracts people nearly around the clock, especially on long summer nights. Nearby sights include the Domkirke, a seventeenth-century church whose tower is a convenient reference point for tourists and locals alike; the National Theater; the National Gallery, which houses many of the greatest masterpieces of Norwegian art; and the main buildings of the university.

Dominating the opposite side of the harbor from the Akershus is the Aker Brygge. This controversial new complex of shops, restaurants, and offices incorporates some old shipyard buildings into a light and airy concoction of glass and metal. A walkway between the buildings and the harbor is lined with food stalls and other vendors, and is the best spot for people-watching in the city.

Perhaps the most noticeable thing about Oslo, however, is its open spaces. The island of Bygdøy contains a large area of farmland owned by the royal family. Cows grazing in open fields and barns displaying the royal crest above the door, as well as ever present joggers and bicyclists, are common sights for residents and visitors to the many famous museums on Bygdøy, such as the Viking, the Kon Tiki, and the Norsk Folkemuseum. In central Oslo is Vigelandsparken, part of the even larger Frognerparken, home to a world famous sculpture garden by Norway's greatest sculptor, Gustav Vigeland. Outside the city are vast stretches of forest, dotted with rivers, lakes, and mountain meadows. To the north lies Nordmarka, a popular region for hiking or skiing on the marked trails between *hytter*, which are cabins meant for use by hikers and skiers. The Nordmarka is also the home of the famous Holmenkollen ski jump, the world's oldest, whose gentle curve upward toward the sky can be seen from most points in Oslo. Holmenkollen is a national symbol, and an apt one, not just because it combines Norwegians' building skills dating from the Viking era with their equally legendary athletic skills, but also because it shows Norwegian determination to make both work and play part of daily life.

2

THE LAND OF THE VIKINGS

In southern Norway, rock drawings dating from 1500 B.C. to 500 B.C. show human figures using plows drawn by oxen. Other figures hold swords and are mounted on horses. As many as thirty faces stare out from boats. The presentation by the makers of these drawings of both land and sea, their familiarity with both peace and war, and their interest in the world beyond their horizons show that many important elements of Norwegian identity have been present for several millennia. Clearly, by the time these drawings were made, the people who lived in the land known today as Norway already had a distinct identity and way of life, and as the centuries passed, this identity continued to evolve. The country has alternated between periods of isolation and world outreach, between domination and being dominated—all of which has ended up shaping the Norway of today.

EARLY HISTORY

Priceless relics such as these rock drawings provide today a glimpse of life in a region then still a thousand years from developing a written record. Other much older evidence, such as weapons and farming implements carved from animal bones or chipped from flint, suggests that the actual beginnings of Norwegian culture lie even further back in time, around the end of the last Ice Age, approximately twelve thousand years ago. As the ice retreated and the weather actually became somewhat warmer than it is today, dry land emerged along the coastline. People could move up and down the long, narrow shores, settling wherever they thought they could survive.

Of these earliest inhabitants little is known, but archaeological evidence is a bit more substantial for two groups who came much later, around 3000 B.C. They are known today as the Boat-Ax and Battle-Ax peoples, distinguished from each other by the shape of their weapons. These two groups, particularly the Battle-Ax people (who created the rock paintings) seem to have played particularly important roles in the region because their knowledge of agriculture and raising farm animals was instrumental in the establishment of the first permanent communities. The end result of the arrival of these two new groups was a blending of their cultures and a sharing of knowledge and practices among all those inhabiting the region.

Life was hard so far north, and cooperation was essential to survival. As writers Jules Brown and Phil Lee point out in *Norway: The Rough Guide,* newcomers did not tend to try to "overwhelm their predecessors; the two groups co-existed, each picking up hints from the other—a reflection of the harsh infertility of the land."[7] Then, around 500 B.C., the climate, always a central force in Norway, for some unknown reason suddenly became much colder. According to historian Rowlinson Carter, "Survival in the new Ice Age demanded cultural adjustments."[8] Most of those people who were still semi-nomadic—living outside of the small villages which dotted the coastline and fertile valleys—had to cut back their wandering, and instead build sturdy homes which could withstand the winter and also grow crops to keep themselves alive through the cold months of darkness.

Generally ignored by a Europe preoccupied with its own wars and power struggles, Norwegians for many centuries kept largely to themselves, mostly on small isolated farms

GARLANDS AND GIANT EARS

Norway was a place shrouded in legend long before the Vikings burst onto the European scene and focused attention on this mysterious land to the north. One ancient Roman writer, Pomponius Mela, claimed that the people of Norway lived on bird eggs and had hoofed feet. Their ears were said to be so large they pulled them around their bodies to use as clothing. An ancient Greek legend said that the region was home to the Hyperboreans, a people who lived a life of great ease, singing and dancing in the forest. They did not get old, but when they grew tired of living, they covered themselves with flower garlands and flung themselves from cliffs.

and villages. Cultural and technological advantages which contact with the outside world might have brought, such as the development of a written language, were slow in coming. It was not until approximately 200 A.D. that alphabet characters called runes, roughly modeled after Greek and Roman letters, were first used in Norway. Likewise, although raw materials for making iron were present in large quantities in Norway's marshes and bogs, people did not begin smelting "bog iron" until the fifth century A.D., long after most other European cultures had done so.

Two Leaps Forward

Production of iron tools brought about two results that would have a profound effect on Norwegian life in the centuries that followed. First, iron axes made clearing forests easier, enabling people to farm in more areas. Because the soil is not particularly fertile in Norway and the growing season is short, a farm had to be fairly large to support a family. Once iron tools were available to help with the job, "family homesteads leapfrogged up the valleys."[9] Because no noble class had evolved, unlike many other places in Europe, farms remained wide apart instead of clustering around castles. In fact, castles were almost nonexistent in Norway, and even villages were few and far between. The average Norwegian farm family had only a few neighbors within visiting distance and little contact with the outside world. Many social historians have pointed out that this fact profoundly affected Norwegian culture, creating a self-reliant, unpretentious people, who tend to see others not as their inferiors or superiors but simply as fellow strugglers and sharers of a time and place.

During this early era certain individuals were able to exercise enough power within a small area to be regarded as chieftains, but their power was a matter of individual strength of personality, and was not based on hereditary right or on ownership of all the land they claimed power over. Chieftains were routinely killed if their popularity waned or if their followers simply wanted to switch allegiance to someone else. Historical records of an early group of chieftains survive in a poem entitled *Ynglinga Tal,* written by Tjodolf, and show the precariousness of chieftains' lives: "Domaldi was sacrificed to ensure the fertility of his land; Dag was killed . . . by a pitchfork, and Fjolnir got up in the night to take a leak, fell into a vat of mead [honey wine] and drowned."[10] Another chieftain, Half-dan the Black, was chopped to pieces and the pieces buried all over his lands. Like Domaldi's, his body itself was a sacrifice to ensure fertility of the lands. Most people, however, took little notice of such gruesome events. Individuals simply went about their lives tending their animals and crops, spinning their wool, baking their bread and churning their butter, caring for the living and burying the dead.

Ironmaking made independent farming possible for many Norwegians, but it had a second far reaching effect as well. Boat building was easier with iron tools and hardware. A boat in excess of fifty feet in length, perfectly preserved for more than a thousand years in a bog near Hammerfest in northern Norway, demonstrates that ships big enough to survive long open sea voyages were built as early as the seventh century. Another boat found in a burial mound in southern Norway is even larger. Eighty-two feet long by sixteen feet wide, it had a sailing mast and also sixteen sets of oars. A steering board (from which the nautical term "starboard" originated) was on its right side and

Built as early as the seventh century, boats such as this one allowed Norwegians to travel long distances. Boats have been found as large as eighty-two feet long and sixteen feet wide.

the board could be pulled up for beach landings. A modern copy of the Gokstad ship, as this boat is known, took less than a month to cross the Atlantic on a recent demonstration voyage. Historical accounts claim that some ancient Norwegian ships could hold as many as a thousand people. Though by no means the first culture to take to the seas, the early Norwegians were unique in that their ships were designed to take them well out to sea for long periods. Other explorers, such as the ancient Phoenicians, traveled long distances but generally stayed within sight of land.

THE VIKINGS

These boats show that while the rest of Europe paid no attention, the people of Norway were developing maritime skills and technology which would soon make them the most powerful seafarers in the western world. As Rowlinson Carter points out, "These ships represented a menacing mobility, and once the Norwegians had cause to take their unsuspecting neighbors to the south by surprise, they were able to do so with stunning efficiency."[11]

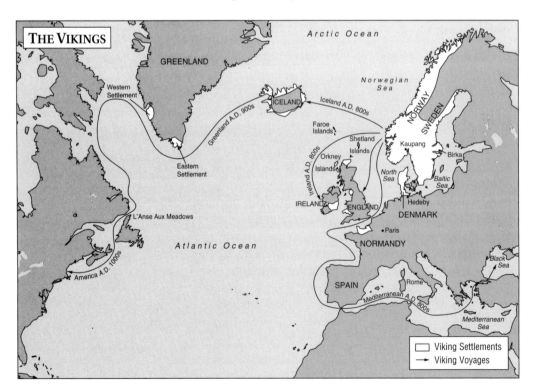

Theories abound as to why the first Vikings, as these seafarers were known, suddenly burst upon the world in 793 A.D. with their plunder of the monastery at Lindesfarne, in northern England. The simplest explanation seems to be that Norway could no longer support its population, particularly young adult men. Although the system of inheritance allowed farms to be split among several heirs, there was no point in dividing land if the resulting farms were too small to support a family. Hence, sons not able or willing to become farmers needed some use for their time and some means of making a livelihood. Under the leadership of local chieftains, bands of Vikings, originating from Norway, Sweden, or Denmark, reached as far south as Seville in Spain, as far east as Constantinople (now Istanbul) in Turkey, and as far west as North America. These men—and the occasional woman, such as the leader known as the Red Maiden, who commanded a Viking army in Ireland—were the most feared people in all of the western world.

A CRUEL CODE OF ETHICS

This fear was well founded, for the Vikings were ruthless, bloodthirsty killers and plunderers. Their code of ethics was simple. People were not entitled to either their life or their property, so both could be taken at will and without remorse. Children were run through with swords, women were raped, and buildings were burned during the course of Viking raids. The Vikings' legendary cruelty and bravery in combat were an asset. As they traveled further from home on raids which historian Rowlinson Carter says "were conducted like annual summer holidays,"[12] the Vikings found their reputation had preceded them. Sometimes villages would be deserted when they arrived, the inhabitants having fled to safety, leaving their valuables behind to keep from being followed. Other times, Viking bands were offered money to stay away. For example, after sacking Paris in 857 and again in 861, the Vikings were offered three thousand pounds of silver by the French king, Charles the Bald, to go plunder someone else instead. They took the silver but came back in 885, prepared to sack the city again if they did not receive more silver. They left the city intact after receiving another seven hundred pounds of silver.

Vikings, despite the cruelty of their methods, did not make war for its own sake, and in fact the majority of them stayed

DISCOVERING THE NEW WORLD

The Vikings explored widely, and their accomplishments during the two centuries when they did so are legendary. Because records are scanty, and because the terms "Viking," "Dane," "Northman," and "Norseman" tended to be used interchangeably, it is now difficult to know which feats should be attributed to which Viking group. But it is generally accepted that the Swedish Vikings tended to explore eastward, in the direction of Russia, and that the Danish Vikings headed directly south. The Norwegian Vikings were the most daring and far ranging. They headed first for the British Isles, founding Dublin in 836 A.D. Later, some Vikings headed as far south as Spain, while most explored westward from Norway, settling the Hebrides and Shetland Islands before continuing on at sea and discovering Iceland in the early tenth century.

Greenland was discovered by a particularly quarrelsome Viking, Erik the Red. First exiled to Iceland from Norway, Erik was then banished from Iceland after committing a local murder. He set out westward in 985, and soon discovered a new land he named Greenland. Two historical documents written a century later, the *Vinland Sagas,* tell the story of Leif Eriksson, son of Erik the Red, who set off to explore west from Greenland and eventually founded a colony in North America, around 1000 A.D., five hundred years before Columbus set out from Spain. The remains of a Viking community discovered at Anse aux Meadows in the Canadian province of Newfoundland offer proof of the story told in the *Vinland Sagas.* Historians and archaeologists concur that this settlement was populated for nearly five hundred years. The last survivors—who still predated Columbus—died miserably, wracked with disease and under continual attack by the native Inuit population, the settlers' link to Norway broken off permanently by decades of particularly bad weather which precluded them making the voyage home.

Trondheim harbor is home to this statue of Leif Eriksson, a Viking explorer who founded a colony in North America around A.D. 1000.

home and farmed. Those who set sail were in essence professional warriors, and Viking raiding parties looked for the
same things businesspeople look for today—maximum
profit with minimum risk. The Vikings were first and fore-
most interested in plundering poorly guarded places, such as
monasteries, where they expected to find gold crosses, jew-
eled chalices, and other valuables. If locals mounted a successful resistance to Viking attack, as in Wales in 795, the
raiders simply moved on to an easier target. The Vikings did
more than simply rob and steal valuables, however, although
that clearly was their preferred labor. According to Rowlinson Carter,

> When the Vikings came across unoccupied land, or . . .
> rendered it so by annihilating the natives, they were
> keen to settle it. If that proved to be impractical, a raid
> might at least produce some slaves who could either be
> sold, or, increasingly, put to good use at home. When
> piracy could not be made to pay, however, the Vikings
> were willing to engage in conventional trade.[13]

THE VIKING LEGACY

The Vikings, despite their fearsome reputation, achieved
more than the burning of buildings and the emptying of trea-
suries. They had a positive, although somewhat ironic, overall effect on Norway. Vikings saw clearly that it was one thing
to rob strangers in far away places, but it was quite another
thing to be subject to the same possibility at home. Rules
were clearly needed to protect Viking property and lives from
other Vikings! Thus, it is during the Viking era that the first
codes of law were established in Norway.

Given the violence of the Viking culture, it is no real surprise that the focus of the first law, called *wergild*, was on the
compensation owed to survivors of a murdered person.
Other laws also showed the mercilessness of the Viking culture, including the law establishing that a slave owner was
guilty of no crime if his slaves died of exhaustion or abuse. Yet
another law declared it permissible to throw children of a
dead slave into an open grave to die from exposure to the elements. Oddly, the same law required that the owner of the
dead slave monitor such disposal, because he *was* obligated
to save the last child.

Any system of law, however perverse it might seem and however unjust the purposes it serves, is nevertheless an important early step in the establishment of a unified society. Without laws, a leader's influence usually does not spread far beyond his or her physical presence, and people do not develop the trust that fosters interdependence among far-flung communities. Thus, though their laws reflected an attitude that the Vikings would continue behaving in a way that required punishment, the Vikings nevertheless, by establishing those laws, set in motion the eventual development of Norway into a unified, modern nation.

SOCIAL ORGANIZATION

Viking laws were established through an institution known as the *lagting*. Although historians agree, as one notes, that "general assemblies . . . must have met throughout the country in prehistoric times for dealing with . . . matters of common concern,"[14] it is in the Viking era, during the reign of Harald Hårfagri, around 900 A.D., that the first records appear of meetings of a general assembly in which all free men could participate. This assembly was called the *ting*. A second body, the *lagting*, was a group of "specially appointed men [who] met on behalf of the local peasant communities"[15] to make laws and function as a court.

New laws and a system of assembly were only two of the signs that the Viking era brought a general increase in social organization. It took a great deal of planning and strong leadership to mount a Viking expedition, and according to historian Knut Herne, "Some of the early Norwegian kings built their power on the basis of their experience as Vikings."[16] Furthermore, Herne adds, their past and intended victims in Europe and elsewhere had to become more socially organized as well. "Provoked by Viking invasions, many areas were forced to consolidate power in order to resist."[17] One additional effect of the Viking era was the exposure of the Vikings themselves to the cultures and goods of regions to the south. Herne explains that the Vikings "learned useful lessons in political organization from those abroad they hoped to subjugate. Furthermore, these organizations produced wealth and greater military know-how, which the Viking chieftains used to their advantage upon returning home."[18]

Viking expeditions also set in motion the development of trade and expansion of agriculture. By the goods, stolen or

NORSE MYTHOLOGY

The Vikings had their own mythology, which has been handed down in a work known as the *Poetic Edda,* dating from the eighth century A.D. It survived only because of copies in Viking settlements in Iceland. All the Norwegian versions were destroyed over the centuries. The *Poetic Edda* consists of thirty-four narrative poems called *lays,* which describe the antics and personalities of the Norse gods and goddesses.

The chief god was Odin, who governed poetry and magic as well as war and wisdom. He was not king of the gods although he had the most influence among them. Odin was, to quote Jules Brown and Phil Lee, in *Norway: The Rough Guide,* "untrustworthy, violent, and wise in equal measure." He presided at Valhalla, a hall where dead heroes were brought to spend eternity, sated with good wine and food, and served by warrior maidens called Valkyries. Odin was said to have created the world and the tree of life which sustains it; but the tree of life was beyond his control after its creation. The word Wednesday comes from the German variant of Odin's name, Woden, and means "Woden's day."

Thor was the god of thunder and lightning, which he caused with his magical hammer named Mjolnir. He was the most commonly worshipped of all the Norse gods. The word Thursday means "Thor's day." He was a giant, tremendously strong but also short tempered.

Frey was the third most important god, the god of fertility. He was said to have a magic sword strong enough to carry all the gods, but enchanted so that he could fold it up and place it in his pocket. A goddess with a similar name, Freya, was the goddess of fertility, love, and healing. The word Friday means "Freya's day."

Another important mythological figure was the devious trickster, Loki. His actions made Loki the enemy of the other gods, who chained him underneath a serpent that dripped venom onto his face. Loki's squirming was said to cause earthquakes.

The chief god of Norse mythology, Odin, was believed to govern poetry, magic, war, and wisdom.

otherwise, which Vikings brought back from their voyages, they were able to lay the seeds for development of a merchant class. Slavery was widespread, and Irish and other slaves helped clear the Norwegian interior for larger farms, on which the slaves then labored. Opportunities to trade agricultural surpluses for luxury goods brought back from Europe and elsewhere contributed to a higher standard of living for the Vikings, though that standard was generally not shared by the slaves themselves.

THE RISE OF A UNITED NORWAY

Improvements in the standard of living and the development of the first law codes are not the only legacies of the Vikings. During the two centuries of Viking dominance, the natural competitiveness among warrior chieftains led to a desire to control more and more territory and to get rid of as many rivals as possible. From this manuevering for power among local strongmen emerged a single, larger country. By the middle of the eleventh century, the territory stretching from the southern tip of Norway up through the central west coast region was ruled by an undisputed monarch, Harald Hardråda, "the last of the Viking heroes."[19]

The first of the Viking heroes, however, and the first man to claim a wider base of power than his own immediate valley or fjord was another Harald, called the Fairhaired, or Harald Hårfagri. Around the year 900 A.D., he won a battle over several other Viking chieftains, gaining control of a large stretch of land along the coast. Many of the defeated chieftains decided to move to Iceland, and their withdrawal contributed to Harald's undisputed status as the closest thing to a king of Norway yet seen. Because there was no tradition of kingship, when Harald died all that he had held together by force of his personality and accomplishments threatened to break apart again. Two of Harald Hårfagri's sons, Eirik Bloodax and Håkon the Good, began a power struggle which Eirik's sons joined and which ended only with Håkon's death in battle at the sons' hands in 960.

One of Eirik Bloodax's sons, Harald Greycloak Erickson, took the title of king of Norway, with the assistance of the king of Denmark, Harald Bluetooth, who thought that Harald Greycloak's loyalty to Denmark might thus be secured. Bluetooth was wrong. Once in place as king, Greycloak began distancing himself from his former ally, so much so that

Bluetooth had him murdered and managed to get a Dane, Håkon Sigurdsson, named king of Norway. Sigurdsson turned out to be no more interested in loyal subservience to Bluetooth than was Greycloak, and during Sigurdsson's reign Norway continued to develop a separate national identity.

Two important leaders named Olav continued the development of a united Norway through their efforts to gain the crown for themselves. The first, Olav Tryggvason, was able to gain control over the same region Harald Hårfagri had once dominated. Although Olav was not the first Christian king (Håkon the Good had been converted during a long stay in England), Tryggvason was more successful at converting Vikings—by force or by persuasion—than Håkon had been. Under Olav's rule, converting heathens was used as a justification for brutal wars of subjugation, most notably against the Tronds, the pagan inhabitants of the area around Nidaros, today's Trondheim.

Because of Olav's role in converting the region, later Christian writers painted Tryggvason as being more of a hero than he really was. In the end he was unable to keep the crown for himself or for any other Norwegian. The Danish king, Harald Bluetooth, had died and his son, Svein Forkbeard, wanted to be ruler of Norway as well. Forkbeard joined with Sweden to defeat Olav in battle in the year 1000, and control of Norway was divided between Denmark and Sweden, an arrangement that would repeat itself in varying forms for centuries to come.

King of England and Denmark, Canute the Great also ruled Norway from 1028 until 1035.

The second Olav, Olav Haraldsson, waited in England for the time to be right to make his play for the Norwegian crown. In 1015 his opportunity had arrived. Svein Forkbeard was dead, and his successor, Knut, or Canute, who ruled both Denmark and England, had enough on his hands at the time without worrying about Norway. Olav was able to take the crown, and he became one of the most significant rulers in Norwegian history.

His major claim to fame was completing the conversion of Norway to Christianity. Those unwilling to do so were executed and their pagan places of worship destroyed. Haraldsson was forced from the throne when King Canute successfully invaded Norway in 1028 to regain power. When Olav tried to return to reclaim his throne in 1030 he was killed by an alliance of Viking landowners and chieftains who did not want a return to what they perceived as his heavy-handed use of power. The battle at Stiklestad, where Olav was killed, was the first battle fought on the soil of a united Norway.

The Norwegians soon came to regret their treatment of Olav, because Canute's son Svein, whom he appointed to serve as king of Norway, was equally arrogant and abusive of his power, and in addition, he was not even Norwegian. There was little that could be done about the situation, however, except wait for Canute to die. When that happened, Svein fled, and Olav's young son Magnus became king of Norway.

IN THE WAKE OF THE VIKINGS

The reign of Magnus was largely uneventful and upon his death in 1046 A.D., Olav's half-brother, Harald Hardråda— Harald the Hard—became king. Harald was the perfect embodiment of a Viking warrior king. Seven feet tall with a grand mustache and dramatic eyebrows, Harald Hardråda had a reputation for fearlessness and cruel treatment of enemies that surpassed even the Viking norm. Harald wanted to be a king in the style of Canute, and soon set out to conquer England, in 1066. Outside of York in northern England, he engaged the new English king, Harold Godwinson, in battle and was killed, ending forever Norwegian efforts to conquer England. The effects of Harald Hardråda's English adventure were far-reaching, however, and his most important historical role is that of a spoiler. Distracted by the need to fight Hardråda, the English were unprepared when William the Conqueror arrived in the south of England that same year. After the famous Battle of Hastings, William took the English crown for himself.

After Harald Hardråda, the era of Viking conquest was over. Norway was subsequently ruled by several kings in succession, most notably Håkon IV and Magnus the Lawmender, both of whom are remembered as reigning over Norway's "Period of Greatness." Unlike many other countries, this greatness was not tied to empire building as much as to internal growth and stability. Cathedrals and grand buildings were constructed, and foreign trade increased dramatically. However, a major setback was just around the corner. In 1349, a boat arrived in Bergen carrying bubonic plague, also known as the Black Death. So many people died that crops rotted in the fields and farm animals died in turn, leading to starvation among those who were not killed outright by the plague. The Black Death was a great social equalizer as well, for even the greatest chieftains and their families found themselves victims of starvation or of the disease itself. As these Viking descendants labored in fields, scrambled for crusts of bread, and watched their families die, any ideas they might have had about creating a nobility with grand titles, large armies, huge castles, and vast estates vanished from their minds forever. To this day, Norway is largely devoid of an aristocracy, and a sense of equality is still a source of national pride.

The chaos brought on by the plague resulted in a period of relative political quiet, as few had the strength or the focus to think about who would or should rule Norway. By the time the plague was behind them, Norwegians awoke to the realization that while they had been otherwise occupied, their precious freedom had already vanished.

3

A COUNTRY LOST AND REGAINED

In the 1300s problems with succession to the thrones of Norway, Denmark, and Sweden created a number of situations in which the king of one country became the king of another as well. For example, when Håkon V, the king of Norway, died in 1319 A.D., he left behind no sons. His closest male relative and successor was Magnus Ericsson, the three-year-old son of a Swedish noble. After being crowned king of Norway, Magnus Ericsson was also elected king of Sweden. This shrewd move by Sweden effectively united the two countries under one ruler. It would be five centuries before Norway would reemerge as a completely self-governing country. Although Norway kept its name, and its people were seen as culturally distinct during these centuries, the country was always viewed as backward and second class, a minor part of a larger Scandinavian empire.

MARGARETA AND THE KALMAR UNION

All of Scandinavia was united in 1397 A.D. as a result of the efforts of a Danish princess, Margareta, who had married yet another Norwegian king named Håkon when she was only ten years old. Margareta was perfectly suited to play the manipulative and treacherous games of the royal court, and in later years she persuaded the Danes to accept her half-Norwegian and half-Danish son Olav, then age five, as king of Denmark. When Håkon died, Olav also took over the throne of Norway. Soon afterward, when the Swedish throne was vacant for lack of an heir, Margareta was able to demonstrate Olav's connection to a branch of its royal family, and she secured for him the throne of Sweden as well. Though she never ruled in her own right, Margareta was often addressed as Lady King for the power she wielded behind the scenes on behalf of her son.

Unfortunately for Margareta, Olav died at the age of seventeen, in 1387. Undaunted, she had herself declared regent—or interim ruler—and used her power in this role to get her five-year-old nephew, Erik of Pomerania, chosen as the next king of Sweden, Denmark, and Norway. But Margareta realized that the union she had patched together might not last, so to improve the chances that the dynasty she had founded would be permanent, she decided to have a formal coronation for Erik, symbolically linking the three crowns as one. Tellingly, although the Danish and Swedish archbishops were present and blessed the coronation of Erik, the Norwegians were represented by the lower-ranking bishop of Orkney, which was not even part of Norway itself, but a Viking conquest off the north coast of Scotland. Norway's second class status in the eyes of other Scandinavian nations was apparent already.

The coronation was performed at Kalmar, Sweden, when Erik reached the age of majority in 1397. He reigned for the

The Kalmar Union was formed in 1397, when Erik of Pomerania was crowned king of Norway, Denmark, and Sweden.

next fifty years over what is today called the Kalmar Union. Erik grew increasingly unpopular with the nobles of Sweden and Denmark (there was no significant group of nobles in Norway), however, because to generate income for himself and his court in Copenhagen he squeezed the nobles for more and more money. In addition, he provoked problems with the Hanseatic League, an organization of merchants in northern European port cities, when he tried to force them to pay higher taxes. In response, merchants and nobles together began to plot to remove Erik from the throne. According to writers Jules Brown and Phil Lee, Erik was "incompetent and brutal in equal measure," and "managed to get himself deposed in all three countries at the same time, ending his days as a Baltic pirate."[20]

UNDER THE DANISH HEEL

The Kalmar Union did not continue after Erik. Sweden reasserted itself as a separate monarchy, and Denmark crowned a Danish count, Christian of Oldenburg, as king of Norway and Denmark in 1450 A.D. At this point, although Norway remained separate in name and had its own crown (always held jointly with Denmark's by a Danish king), Denmark gradually ceased to consider Norway as having any separate power or rights. Danes held most of the important government positions, and Norwegians were rarely consulted about matters affecting

KNUT ALVSSON

Norway did not accept its subjugation to Denmark completely passively. In 1501–02 A.D., a Swedish-Norwegian noble named Knut Alvsson led an uprising which had widespread support in the area around and between the two most important Norwegian cities, Oslo and Bergen. The Danish army was sent in to put down the revolt against oppressive taxation and the demeaning treatment of Norwegians by the Danish monarchs.

Alvsson, who had made his headquarters at Akershus, a castle in Oslo, was invited to negotiate a settlement to the rebellion. When he showed up at the meeting where a truce was to be discussed, Alvsson was murdered.

Henrik Ibsen, the great Norwegian playwright, in a poem entitled "At Akershus," called the murder of Alvsson a blow to Norway's heart. Alvsson is viewed as a national hero today.

them, including the disposition of Norwegian territory. One event that particularly galled the Norwegians was Denmark's sale of the Orkney and Shetland Islands, which were Norwegian territories, as a means of raising a dowry for Christian's daughter.

Over the course of the next century, Danish kings whittled away at the few remaining elements of Norwegian identity. Norway's dominant Catholic faith was abolished in favor of the Protestantism favored by the Danes, and many of Norway's Catholic bishops were exiled or killed. More humiliating still, in 1536 Christian III issued an edict proclaiming that Norway was no longer a nation but simply a province of Denmark, "and it shall henceforth neither be nor be called a kingdom in itself."[21] The Norwegian National Council, a body which little by little had been stripped even of a strong advisory role, was abolished altogether. But, as historian Knut Helle points out, "Norway was . . . geographically too large and distant . . . and tradition and the Norwegian sense of identity were sufficient to ensure that Norway continued to be treated as something other than [just] a Danish province."[22]

THREE CENTURIES OF UNION WITH DENMARK

The following three centuries of Danish rule saw a decline of Norwegian culture, tradition, and even language. Though there were some exceptions—most notably Christian IV, who actually visited Norway more than thirty times—Danish rulers took little interest in their western "province." They saw Norway mostly as a source of exploitable raw materials such as fish and lumber, not as a place in need of economic support and development. Danish merchants were permitted to gouge Norwegian fishermen, shopkeepers, and other businesspeople mercilessly by manipulation of prices. For example, fishermen of the Lofoten Islands in the far north had to buy supplies from Danish merchants, who set the price at whatever level they wished. The fishermen were not permitted to set the price for their fish in return, but instead had to accept whatever price the Danes were willing to pay.

Some good things occurred during the Danish era, however. Overall, trade increased and new towns and cities were founded. Oslo was rebuilt after burning to the ground in 1624. Schools were founded and literacy improved. Still,

PIETISM

In 1536 A.D., King Christian III, ruler of both Denmark and Norway, declared that from then on the Lutheran church would be the only one allowed in Norway. This decision was part of a process designed to destroy a separate Norwegian identity (which at that time was devoutly Catholic) so that the people of Norway would in time consider themselves Danes. Norwegians saw through this ploy and resisted wholeheartedly, but eventually came to embrace the new faith.

By the 1700s, many Norwegians had embraced Pietism, a popular form of Protestantism characterized by extremely strict self-discipline and self-denial. Many people felt the state church had become too focused on material things—such as erecting places of worship with fancy steeples, organs, and stained glass—and that this materialism was seeping into people's daily lives and turning them away from God. In "The 400 Year Sleep," historian Rowlinson Carter writes, "the rural areas especially embraced Pietism, real hellfire-and-brimstone stuff which persuaded peasants that their austere existence was actually abominably frivolous."

Pietists were able to get laws enacted making attendance at church and strict observance of the Sabbath compulsory. They frowned on activities which existed simply for pleasure, such as drinking alcohol, and made any sexual contact other than between married couples punishable by death. Pietist missionaries, particularly Thomas von Westen, even had some success converting the Sami to Christianity, though less skilled missionaries often were killed in the process.

By the time Pietism had run its course, most of Norway's traditional wooden stave churches, covered with pagan symbols, had been destroyed. Only a handful remain today, and other priceless artifacts from the pre-Christian and Catholic eras were lost forever in the Pietists' zeal to save souls.

many of these developments had a bitter edge. Oslo was rebuilt, but it was renamed Christiania, in honor of the Danish king. In schools the language of instruction was Danish, and speaking Norwegian was not allowed at all. For many generations, few knew how to write a language they could only speak among themselves, and spoken Norwegian came to resemble Danish more and more. In these and other ways,

Danes and Norwegians alike were encouraged to view everything Danish as sophisticated and superior—and everything
Norwegian as primitive and unworthy of respect.

THE END OF DANISH RULE

The end of Danish rule over Norway came about as a result
of a struggle between France and Britain. About 1800, Denmark had sided against Great Britain in a long and bloody
European war. When Napoleon came to power as emperor of
France, hostilities between Denmark and Great Britain were
still intense, including seizures of ships and harassment at
sea, and Napoleon was thus able to convince the Danes to
support him against Great Britain. Norway, as part of the
Danish kingdom, was thus allied against Great Britain as
well.

   The ensuing conflict was in part economic, in that Danish and Norwegian ports were closed to British vessels. The
great English admiral Lord Nelson sailed to the Danish capital of Copenhagen with a massive fleet to break this trade
embargo. His bombardment of Copenhagen was massive
and effective, forcing the entire Norwegian and Danish fleets
to surrender. Denmark's position worsened after the defeat
of Napoleon in 1814, when under terms of the Treaty of Kiel,
Denmark was forced to cede all of Norway to Sweden—
which had sided with Great Britain. In this way four hundred
years of Danish domination of Norway came to an end.

A DISAPPOINTING NEW UNION

Though many Norwegians were happy to end the relationship with Denmark, the Treaty of Kiel hardly gained the
country any respect. The treaty simply handed Norway from
one foreign power to another. Moreover, the treaty did not
really end Danish meddling in Norway's affairs. The Danish
crown prince, Christian Frederik, unwilling to accept that he
would not be King of Norway as well as of Denmark, went to
Norway to try to fan the flames of discontent against Sweden.
In 1814 Christian Frederik called together an assembly of a
little over one hundred farmers, merchants, businessmen,
and others. This group produced a constitution and a decla-
ration of independence, and also, not incidentally, named
Christian Frederik as king of the newly independent nation.
Christian Frederik's contribution to Norway is recognized in

that the day the constitution was signed, May 17, is still celebrated as the Norwegian Independence Day. Of course, the king of Sweden, Karl XIV Johan, was not at all willing to accept the independence of Norway. He invaded, and Christian Frederik was soon forced to abdicate, but not before he lured Sweden into a treaty by which the Swedes promised to respect the Norwegian constitution and to recognize the Storting, or parliament, as the legitimate governing body of the country.

Karl XIV Johan was actually quite well liked by many Norwegians throughout his reign, largely because he was perceived as an improvement on the Danes. Karl XIV Johan, however, did not fully honor the treaty he had signed, and he and the Storting endured a long period of strife over such issues as whether he could veto legislation, and whether key ministers serving Norway should be Norwegians. Nevertheless, Karl XIV Johan seemed to understand that the best way to secure a continued union of the two nations was to make Norway happy. Giving it more autonomy and helping it prosper economically and grow culturally was the best route to that end. For example, from 1836 on, only Norwegians were appointed to high offices in Norway, and new local governing councils were set up. Many beautiful buildings, including the Karl Johan's Gate and parts of the University of Oslo date from this time, built as signs of the king's interest in Norway.

Karl XIV Johan, the king of Sweden, invaded Norway in 1818 and managed to reign over both nations until his death in 1844.

THE GROWTH OF NORWEGIAN AUTONOMY

Many Norwegians still longed for the full independence they had briefly tasted under Christian Frederik. Members of the Storting launched challenge after challenge to Karl XIV Johan's authority. They demanded their own foreign consulates and diplomats and the right of Norwegian ships to fly their own flag at sea. These might seem like minor points, but they are clear indications of a nation's sovereign status. Karl XIV Johan's refusal to permit such things showed that he viewed Norway only as part of Sweden. Karl XIV Johan's successor, Oskar I, tried to placate the Storting by small gestures such as reversing the order of the kingdoms in his title—"king of Norway and Sweden"—and creating a new flag which equally displayed each country's national colors, but these minor concessions were not what Norway had in mind.

While the Storting tried to limit the king's power, other forces were growing which would change the composition of the Storting itself. Up to this point land owners and merchants had been the only ones who had shown much interest in serving in the Storting. Now small farmers began to understand that they needed to be involved if they wanted their concerns to be heard and their problems addressed. Likewise factory and other workers began organizing politically, and the strong labor movement which still exists today came into being. As the composition of the Storting shifted away from wealthier Norwegians, who might have seen the benefit of continued economic ties with Sweden, toward people who felt they gained nothing from such an arrangement, it soon became clear that the days of union with Sweden were numbered.

Using the long-standing dispute over diplomatic representation abroad as a pretext, the Storting concluded, rather dubiously, that if all its members resigned and no one could be found to serve in their place, the whole Norwegian political structure could be said to have collapsed, taking the monarchy with it. A new Storting could then convene and choose a new king. Improbably, Oskar was convinced that if he stepped down voluntarily, Norwegians would soon ask him to return to solve the problems he was sure that Norwegian self-government would create. In 1905 Oskar abdicated—and spent the rest of his life wondering when he would be asked to return. But Norway never looked back.

Karl XIV Johan's successor, Oskar I, abdicated in 1905 under the mistaken belief that Norwegians would soon ask him to return as their monarch.

A NATION IN TRANSITION

Håkon VII was crowned king of the newly independent constitutional monarchy of Norway, and he ruled over a nation that had already been in transition for some time.

The nineteenth century is often referred to as the Romantic Era, a period when across Europe and the United States artists, writers, and other intellectuals were longing for a return to simpler times. They idealized, among other things, what they perceived as the simple, honest lives of farmers and other rural folk. In Norway, composers such as Edvard Grieg used traditional folk dance melodies in their works, poets wrote about the beauty of nature and life away from the cities, writers extolled national folk heroes, and painters created majestic landscapes.

During the Romantic Era, national and ethnic pride grew in Norway. Linguist and social critic Christopher Bruin was enormously influential in the late nineteenth century for his essays arguing that only by taking pride in their mythology, language, customs, history, and national character could Norwegians stop seeing themselves as secondary and inferior to the other peoples and cultures of Europe. Rural Norwegians, heretofore seen as rough and backward, were elevated to the status of quiet heroes. A new written language, *nynorsk,* was developed to undo what was perceived as the damage of Danish influence on Norwegian speech and literature. The traditional ethnic costume, the *bunad,* became popular dress for weddings, church attendance, and other special events all over Norway.

Reflecting a trend that had swept through Europe during the nineteenth century, the common man became the most important element in Norwegian political life. The era around the beginning of the twentieth century saw in Norway many social reforms benefitting the common man—unemployment relief and improvement in factory conditions, a universal franchise giving both men and women the right to vote, significant expansion of public schools and universities, and the emergence of strong trade unions. But although political disagreements between the newly dominant Labor Party and other political groups often caused strife in the Storting, there was one thing about which most Norwegians agreed: They wanted no further part in anyone else's wars.

WORLD WAR I

When World War I broke out, Norway declared itself neutral, although Norwegians found it difficult to stick to this position. Pressure from both sides resulted in secret deals for the sale of fish and other food to the various warring armies, as well as for use of Norwegian harbors and ships to transport goods, troops, and war supplies. Despite Norway's claim of neutrality, half of its merchant fleet and thousands of lives ended up being lost at sea. In fact, according to Rowlinson Carter, "only Britain lost more of its shipping"[23] as a consequence of the war. Because it had not officially been a combatant, however, Norway was not perceived as a victor when peace was negotiated. Carter points out that "despite its heavy losses the Norwegian merchant navy received no compensation in the shape of ships from the confiscated German navy," as Great Britain and others did, "and it was ten years before injured seamen and the families of those killed received any compensation from the German government."[24]

By the 1920s, Norway still had not recovered from the effects of war and was sinking into an economic depression— which worsened when the United States stock market crashed in 1929 and world markets spiraled downward as well. Labor unrest was growing, as many Norwegians experienced real poverty and fear of the future for the first time. The Russian Revolution had by this time deposed the czar and instituted a communist government in that country. Communism, which advocates ideas such as ownership of factories by the workers, and collective rather than individual labor and profit, was seen by many in the Labor Party as a model for Norway's future, but this political philosophy was vehemently opposed by other Norwegians. Strikes became widespread and occasionally violent, when police and army troops attacked demonstrators. Eventually the Labor Party moved away from its radical communist ideas, and, having widened its appeal in the process, came to power under Prime Minister Johan Nygaardsvold in the late 1930s.

For a brief period, things seemed to be looking up for Norway. By 1938, the depression appeared to be over. People were working again, largely because of public works projects such as highways and railroads, but also because private industries were once again working at full speed. The following year, however, trouble loomed on the southern horizon. World War II had begun.

VIDKUN QUISLING

The word "quisling" to identify a traitor came into use as a result of the actions of Vidkun Quisling, a Norwegian politician in the years before and during World War II.

In 1933 Quisling formed a new party in Norway called the Nasjonal Samling (NS), or National Unification party, similar in its philosophy to that expounded by Adolf Hitler, who was then a rising young politician in Germany. An ardent anti-Semite, Quisling was thrilled to watch Hitler's power grow, and maintained close contacts with Hitler in the years before the breakout of World War II. Quisling even went so far as to propose that Hitler and Benito Mussolini, the Italian leader who held beliefs similar to Hitler's, be awarded the Nobel Peace Prize.

Although Quisling's party never had much support in Norway, with only about fifteen hundred registered members and a handful of seats in the Storting, when Germany occupied Norway during World War II, Hitler tried to install Quisling as prime minister. Failing in that effort, Hitler created a new post, "Minister President," by which Quisling oversaw Nazi efforts in Norway. All but Quisling's NS party were abolished. All children between ten and eighteen were forced to join the Hitler Youth. Resisters were shot or sent to Grini, a concentration camp set up outside Oslo. Quisling was perceived as a traitor to his people, who did not support the Nazi party and who suffered greatly under the Nazi occupation. After the war, Norway held trials for those it considered war criminals. Many were let off with fairly light sentences because it was perceived that their disgrace was enough. Quisling, however, along with two dozen other high level collaborators, was shot.

Later shot as a traitor, Vidkun Quisling headed the Norwegian equivalent of Germany's Nazi Party under Hitler's direction.

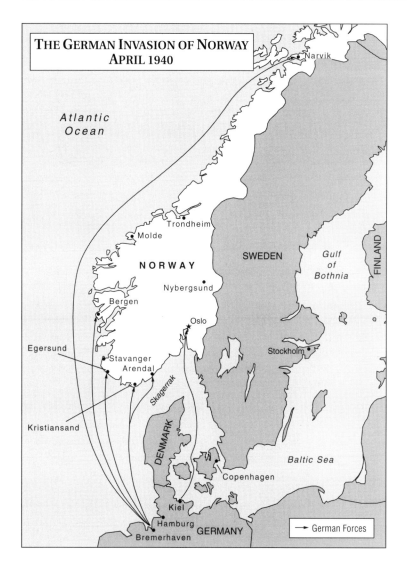

WORLD WAR II

Johan Nygaardsvold was perhaps concentrating too hard on the country's economic revival, for Norway was caught unprepared to defend itself when war broke out. It immediately declared neutrality but soon was faced with problems resulting from skirmishes in its harbors and fjords between German and British ships. Great Britain violated Norwegian neutrality by mining some of its harbors, and on the pretext of defending Norway against such British activity, Nazi Germany invaded Norway in April 1940.

SACRIFICE IN THE SNOW

Jan Baalsrud was part of a sabotage mission in Norway during the Nazi occupation. He escaped an ambush and lived for several months on the run, with help from local people who risked their lives to offer him food and shelter. In this passage from *We Die Alone,* Jan Baalsrud's story, author David Howarth describes how Baalsrud hid in a snow cave for three weeks, suffering from frostbitten feet and watching gangrene spread up his legs.

[His toes] were not part of him any more . . . and it seemed only common sense that he would be better off without them. With the brandy as his anesthetic and [his pocket-knife] as his scalpel, he began carefully to dissect them one by one. It would have been best to get it all over with quickly, but apart from the pain and the sickening repulsion, it was difficult to cut them. He had to find the joints. His hands were rather clumsy and very weak because there had been some frostbite in his fingers too. He grimly persevered. As each one was finally severed, he laid it on the small ledge of rock above him where he could not see it because he no longer had the strength to throw it away. This grisly operation was spread out over nearly three days. At the end of it there were nine toes on the ledge. The little toe on his left foot did not seem so bad . . . so he kept it.

After it was all done, he went back with relief to the simple routine of his daily life: feeding himself, collecting ice water, trying to clean his pistol. It was terribly difficult not to lie there listening, imagining the sound of skis or the distant snarl of wolves. Sometimes he stopped up his ears to keep out the ghastly silence, and sometimes he talked to himself so that there was something to listen to. When people did come from [the village], shouting "Hallo" from far off, the sudden disturbance of the silence was a shock, and it often took him some time to find his voice to answer.

Allied forces came to Norway's aid, and briefly it appeared as if an all-out war would be fought on Norwegian soil to keep the country out of Nazi hands. In northern Norway, battles were fought in the strategic, iron-ore-producing region around Narvik, as well as further south, at the port of Trondheim. Wherever skirmishes broke out along the northern coast, bombers from the Luftwaffe, the German air force, reduced everything to rubble. The Allies were soon diverted to other battlefronts in continental Europe, and Norway was left on its own to deal with what it now feared would be a long-standing Nazi occupation. The king and government went into exile in Great Britain. A Norwegian Nazi named Vidkun Quisling and a German, Josef Terboven, were appointed by Hitler to the two top positions in Nazi-occupied Norway, and a long period of repression began.

The rest of the war in Norway was characterized not by open battles, but rather by local resistance in the form of sabotage and outright refusal to cooperate. The German response to Norwegian resistance was harsh. Often saboteurs and resisters were shot, or else they were sent to a concentration camp, Grini, near Oslo. Not a death camp with gas chambers and crematoria, such as Auschwitz in Poland, Grini nevertheless claimed many prisoners' lives through disease, exposure, hunger, and medical neglect. But sabotage and resistance continued. One famous example is the destruction in 1943 of a plant at Rjukan, in Telemark, where Germans were working on developing "heavy water" to help build an atomic bomb. Another example of resistance was the "Shetland Bus," a secret ferry service which took people to safety in Great Britain and brought saboteurs into Norway. Telavag, near Bergen, was leveled when the Nazis discovered it was a key embarkation point for the Shetland Bus. All the town's residents were deported, interned at Grini, or shot.

REBUILDING NORWAY

When the tide of the war turned against the Nazis, they began retreating from northern Norway, adopting a "scorched earth" policy of burning and blowing up everything behind them. Many of the towns along the coast were completely destroyed, but following the war, Norwegians quickly rebuilt. The typical northern Norwegian town today is a mix of buildings in traditional styles and of generally ugly construction rapidly thrown together after the war. Still, the reestablishment of sizable towns at all was a sign of the Norwegian desire to get back to normal as quickly as possible.

This rapid rebuilding is also a sign of something at the core of Norwegian character. Other people might look at a blown-up town in a hostile, Arctic environment and tell themselves it is time to move. But Norwegians value their far-flung communities and rural lifestyle, and instead focused not just on rebuilding, but on making life better for people living far away from major population centers. Post war developments in Norway have included transportation systems and other improvements that have made it possible for people to stay where they traditionally have lived, but still participate more fully in the life of the nation and improve their standard of living. No matter how remote one's farmstead may have been, it almost certainly had

GRO HARLEM BRUNDTLAND

From the time of the Vikings, leaders in Norway have been almost exclusively men. Even a royal daughter has never become the ruling monarch. Thus, it was a major milestone for Norway when, in 1981, Dr. Gro Harlem Brundtland was selected as Norway's first woman prime minister. This accomplished woman was only forty-one when she took office.

Under Brundtland, things were definitely not business as usual. Seven of the eighteen cabinet members in her Labor Party administration were women—a record unsurpassed in the rest of the world. Capable of building consensus among a wide range of political groups, Brundtland was generally felt to be an effective leader, but falling oil prices created a number of problems such as increased unemployment and tax hikes for which she was blamed. When her government was voted out, she lost her position as prime minister; but within a few years she was back in office. With only one short interruption Brundtland served as prime minister for ten more years between 1986 and 1996, when she stepped down, in part over her disappointment at being unable to persuade Norway to join the European Union.

Since she left office Brundtland has served as director general of the World Health Organization. An ardent environmentalist, she is also known as the author of "Our Common Future," a 1987 United Nations report calling for the world to adopt economic policies which avoid harming the environment. This publication is often referred to as the Brundtland Report.

After serving as prime minister in Norway twice between 1981 and 1996, Gro Harlem Brundtland served as director general of the World Health Organization.

electricity within a decade or so of the end of the war. Farmers began to be heavily subsidized to make staying on their farms possible. Schooling through the university level soon became available in even small northern cities such as Tromsø.

Much of the rebuilding, and the equal emphasis on the needs of rural and urban Norwegians, was the result of the moderate socialism of the Labor Party, whose belief in "an equal society and care for all"[25] produced a post war nation where a strong central government controls much of industry and provides excellent comprehensive social services. In essence, Norway's political and economic philosophy is that individuals are responsible for earning a living through their own efforts, but in return for paying a third or more of their earnings in taxes, they are assured of health care, education, and an adequate income if they fall ill, lose their jobs, or reach retirement age. Though the last few decades have seen the decline of the Labor Party's popularity, it is clear the Labor Party has done the most to shape modern Norway. In recent years, however, a general sense of unease about the ability of the state to meet the needs of all Norwegians has caused debate about the future of Norwegian socialism.

"ALL FOR NORWAY"

While supporting its own people, Norway has also taken on a leading role on the world stage in regard to such key issues as protection of the environment, human rights, and support for developing third world nations. Norway has been an active member of the United Nations and of NATO for many years. Still, Norwegians fear giving up any of their autonomy, and recently a national referendum narrowly voted down joining the European Union. It is clear that on most issues Norway is more than comfortable going its own way.

Norway's future, like every country's, is uncertain, and, like it or not, that future is not entirely in Norway's own hands to decide. But the nation is rich in resources, with a well-educated population that tends to make decisions thoughtfully and with the greater good of all its people in mind. Norwegians are deeply patriotic, shown not in aggression towards others but in a desire to live in and participate in building the best possible Norway. The motto of the royal family is "All for Norway," and this motto echoes the sentiments of the citizenry as well. Whatever the future holds, Norwegians are certain to make the best of it.

4

Norwegians at Work and Play

Activities in Norway are tied closely to the time of year. They are also linked to whether one lives in a city or on a farm, on the coast or inland, in the Arctic Circle or in the south. In spite of location, however, there are certain elements of life that remain the same for all Norwegians. Children go to school, adults go to work and maintain their homes, and nearly everyone participates in the social, athletic, and cultural activities which many Norwegians see as the backbone of their national identity.

Norway Through the Year

Although there are regional differences, all of Norway is profoundly affected by the seasons. In the fall, when the country is bathed in the golden, fading light of the sun, families enjoy one last picnic or take one last hike before the snow falls. Even in towns which would be considered wilderness outposts by American standards, Norwegians feel a need to get away from the local streets and noise to breathe even fresher air and enjoy the solitude. They may visit their *hytte,* or cabin, to collect cloudberries for making jam, or pull out their skis to make any needed repairs. Children go back to school, and adults make final preparations for a winter of scant light and constant cold. By November there is a good cover of snow, and long hours are spent indoors as daylight decreases and temperatures fall. Still, there is always activity in the streets of the towns and cities, and playgrounds remain full of children bundled against the cold.

For several months in winter, temperatures remain well below freezing in much of Norway, and the sun is visible for only a few hours, just above the horizon. The end of the long winter is signaled by the lengthening of daylight hours, the breaking up of ice on lakes and streams, and the appearance of brown patches on the mountain slopes as the snow melts. Adults begin thinking about how they will spend their summer weekends, and young people look forward to the end of school. Windows are opened, and the winter staleness is let

HYTTER: A NATIONAL INSTITUTION

Norwegian love of the out of doors is shown not just by their involvement in sports but by their going to a *hytte,* a vacation home in a remote location. One in four Norwegians owns a *hytte,* and most others have access to one through friends or their workplace or sports club. A *hytte* may range from a small, refurbished fisherman's cottage on a fjord to a cabin in a valley. It may be without running water or indoor plumbing, or be more luxurious and larger than the cramped city apartment that is the family's primary residence. Whatever its size or level of luxury, the *hytte* is considered an essential element to having a fulfilling life.

Norwegians also make use of a national system of cabins run by Den Norske Turistforeningen (DNT). These cabins are resting points along a vast network of walking trails throughout the country but are found primarily in the area between Oslo, Bergen, and Trondheim. Hikers can set out on any DNT trail and know that they will have a place to spend the night. The lodges range from small rustic establishments where hikers prepare food they have brought themselves, to large facilities with over one hundred beds, hot showers, and a restaurant.

Nearly all Norwegians take advantage of lodges such as this one, known as hyttes.

out. Ice which has turned a soccer field into a skating rink melts, and the soccer balls come out again. Finally summer arrives in full, and Norwegians take to the countryside to pursue outdoor activities such as camping, boating, and fishing. They bask in the sunlight, and swim in lakes, taking advantage of the long summer days, when it is still light at eleven in the evening and light again by three or four in the morning.

THE SPORTING LIFE

Ask any Norwegian what he or she likes to do at any time of year, and the answer will almost always include mention of a sport or a wide range of them. Watching soccer matches and attending skiing and other competitions are popular, but more often Norwegians want to be directly involved in the action. Much of the social life of Norway revolves around membership in organizations devoted to a particular sport, and the typical Norwegian is active in more than one such club. Team sports generally require club membership, but even individual sports draw people together. According to author Michael Brady,

Norwegians have a passion for sports, so much of their free time revolves around physical activities.

Approximately half of the country's 1.4 million families with children are involved in sports in some way [in addition to] direct participation. Father is an official of the local club, and mother helps on the stalls at the annual club flea market. The older children sell club lottery tickets. In fact the whole family helps to run the annual club meets. Most families have one member who is either a certified coach or in training to become one.[26]

Norwegians, young and old, have a passion for playing team sports such as ice hockey and a variant, *bandy*, played with a ball. Soccer is the most popular team sport, however, with over a quarter of a million Norwegians participating in eighteen hundred different amateur clubs. There are twelve thousand sports centers scattered across the country, ranging from simple playing fields to elaborate multi-use sports arenas.

Taking advantage of the mountainous countryside, the most popular individual sport in Norway is skiing in its various forms.

Norwegians also enjoy individual sports, such as hiking and sailing, whether doing them alone or with others. By far the most popular individual sport is skiing in its various forms. There are over fifteen hundred clubs nationwide with a total membership of two hundred thousand. Cross-country skiing is a major winter pastime, as are downhill skiing and racing. Ski-jumping and biathlon (a combination of cross-country skiing and target shooting) are also widely enjoyed. In the summer, the emphasis for many people switches to water sports. According to Michael Brady, "On summer evenings, Oslo fjord is alive with boats, a pattern repeated everywhere. Although Norwegians are said to grow up on skis, messing about in boats is equally ingrained."[27]

Norwegians make a distinction between activities falling under the term *sport*, and those falling under the term *idrett*. *Idrett* is the term for strenuous sports which author Michael Brady describes as "reserved for events in which the limits in performance are determined by the capabilities of the human body."[28] Thus, ice fishing is *sport* but not *idrett*, whereas

SONDRE NORHEIM AND HIS SKIS

Given the Norwegian passion for outdoor activities, many people imagine that their use of skis is very ancient. Although for centuries Norwegians got around their snowy country by walking on boards attached to their boots, it wasn't until the mid-nineteenth century, according to author Robert Spark, in *Insight Guide: Norway,* that

> an eccentric farmer named Sondre Norheim [turned] the pedestrian business of plodding about in snow on two planks into the sport of skiing. His discovery of the delights that could be achieved with planks that were properly shaped and had heel bindings made him overlook his domestic chores. It is apparently true that, when he ran out of firewood in winter, he simply hacked off another piece of his house and put that on the fire.

Norheim discovered that a flexible, bent shape for the ski, and a binding that allowed the heel to move up and down, enabled him to move quickly and easily across country and downhill, and would even enable him to jump off ledges and land safely on his feet. He and his followers in the Telemark area of southern Norway developed a deep knee-bend turn when moving quickly downhill that today is still called the Telemark turn. After Norheim and friends traveled on skis the more than one hundred miles between their village and Oslo, interest in the innovation grew, especially after the first-ever ski-jumping contest, held in Oslo in 1879. Ski schools opened, competitions spread, and within a few decades the recreational and competitive sport of skiing seemed as if it had been around forever.

skiing is *idrett.* Furthermore, the word *aktiv* (active) is often applied to *idrett* activities, indicating that the person is involved competitively. Thus, according to Brady, if a Norwegian at a ski lodge accessible only by skis is asked if he or she is what in English would simply be called "a skier," the response is likely to be "No, I'm a bank clerk. Who me? Never dream of it."[29] To a Norwegian, calling oneself a skier would imply being competitive at a very high level.

The passion for sports is apparent in many ways all over Norway. Statues of sports legends such as marathoner Grete Waitz and skater Sonja Henie are prominently displayed in Oslo, and there is a statue at Oslo's Holmenkollen ski jump

site of King Olav V cross-country skiing with his dog. The ma-
nia for sports is illustrated by a cartoon during a recent election. A politician is portrayed promising more pay and fewer
taxes (both big issues in Norway), but the audience only
looks bored. They jump up in excitement, however, when he
says, "With our party in power, I promise you that Norway
will take first, second, and third at the next Holmenkollen."[30]
The perceived quality of their sports sections is a major factor affecting sales of newspapers, and new high-rise apart-
ments are required by law to include space for storing sports
gear. The Ministry of Church and Education has a special division of "Youth and Idrett," and Norwegian television has as
much sports coverage as networks in the United States carry.

The government is actively involved in promoting sports. An
agency known as the Norges Idrettsforbund (NIF), encompas-
sing fifty-three separate sports federations with over 1.7 million
registered members, receives 90 percent of its funding from tax
revenues, and sports activities receive a third of the profits from
state-run gambling operations such as betting pools and lot-
teries. Thanks in part, no doubt, to such support, Norway has
won more Winter Olympic medals than any other country except the former Soviet Union—a remarkable accomplishment
considering Norway's relatively small population.

This statue of King Olav V cross-country skiing with his dog, located at Oslo's Holmenkollen ski jump, reflects the Norwegian passion for sports.

SCHOOL

Life, however, is not all play for Norwegian youth. Sooner or later children must take off their skis or put away their soccer balls, and get down to the business of learning. The school year begins in mid-August and goes through the middle of June. Children begin school at age six, recently lowered from age seven. Ten years of schooling are compulsory, after which students who are preparing for the university or who want to learn a skilled trade study for another three years in what is called a gymnasium, actually an upper secondary school similar to an American high school.

Compulsory schooling is divided into primary and lower secondary stages, both of which are provided by law free of charge to all inhabitants of Norway. Textbooks are not provided, however, and must be bought unless they can be handed down or borrowed (which is usually possible). If a child is not enrolled in a public or private school, the child's parents are required by law to teach him or her at home. Despite how far apart farms are, and how small the average rural community is, Norway is committed to providing schooling near every child's home. Thus, in order to avoid making students travel great distances to larger schools, Norway has more than one grade level per classroom in approximately a third of its schools, and some schools have only a half-dozen students.

In cities and larger towns, where schools have sufficient students to avoid mixing grade levels in a classroom, an effort is made to keep the same group of children together through the first six years of school. Doing so is considered good for their socialization although it is made more difficult by the differing academic abilities of the students. According to author Elizabeth Su-Dale,

> No special privileges are granted to exceptional students. While slow learners are given additional assistance to make the grade, students who are above average are not encouraged to surpass the normal grade and develop at their own accelerated pace.[31]

Repeating or skipping a year is not allowed. Also, according to Su-Dale, "In primary school there are no marks or examinations. It is believed that children learn best without pressure."[32] This approach reflects Norway's emphasis on alikeness rather than on difference; it is considered unforgivable to behave as if anyone were better or worse than anyone else.

This sense that no one is better than anyone else also is reflected in the respect shown to pupils by teachers and school administrators. Even in the lower grades, children are involved in decisions about their own education. As Oddvar Vormeland, former Director General of the Norwegian Ministry of Education, and Chief Officer of Education in Oslo points out,

> right from the start of school, pupils meet together with their parents to discuss their own situation and development with their respective teachers. This not only means more openness and frankness between pupils, teachers, and parents, but will hopefully foster responsibility and fairness as well.[33]

RUSS

When students graduate from upper secondary school, they begin a celebration that lasts for several weeks. Dressed usually in red outfits resembling overalls, their heads topped by a beret, these *russer,* or *russ,* are granted many liberties during this period. They can make a lot of noise almost any time, almost anywhere. They wake up their teachers in the middle of the night, march down streets singing, and paint graffiti (with washable paint) on walls and sidewalks. Schools issue identification cards to denote graduates, who use these cards to gain admission to "*russ*-only" parties, often huge street dances which last all night.

The *russ* are also permitted to poke clean fun at people. For example, if a bookstore owner near the school has been unfriendly in the past, *russ* students might put up a sign saying "buy books from a nicer person." The victim of *russ* pranks is expected to take it all in stride. But pranks must never cross the line into vandalism. Property must not be destroyed, and the safety of the *russ* themselves and others must not be threatened. In a society where people tend to go out of their way to avoid being noticed, the *russ* are a notable exception, a way for the young to let off steam—and for adults, by their goodwill, to acknowledge the *russ* having completed their secondary education.

This spirit of teamwork is also reflected in active Parents' Councils, and in an unusual coordination unit for each school comprised of teacher, parent, staff, and student representatives, as well as the school principal and a member elected by the school board. This coordination unit has broad authority to resolve issues affecting the school.

Children study much the same subjects as children everywhere, but in Norway now there is also a requirement that students learn the culture and history of the Sami, Norway's indigenous people. Additionally, children begin learning a foreign language—almost always English—in the fourth grade. A second and sometimes even a third foreign language may be undertaken later. Immigrants who do not speak Norwegian are accommodated, if possible, by instruction in both their native tongue and Norwegian.

UPPER SECONDARY EDUCATION

High school students in Norway have two options: they can take a vocational track, or choose courses to prepare them for study at a university.

After completing lower secondary school, teenagers who wish to continue in school may do so, or they may leave the classroom forever. Upper secondary school, which is also free of charge, has two emphases—a vocational track emphasizing apprenticeship training, and one preparing the student for university. Students may choose among a dozen

or so areas of study, including general academic subjects, fishing and maritime topics, agricultural subjects, home economics, social sciences, and economics. Older adults who did not complete upper secondary school are also permitted to attend upper secondary classes.

Upper secondary school, like all levels of Norwegian schooling, emphasizes more than just academic or vocational learning. Educator Oddvar Vormeland explains that "according to the law, the upper secondary school should prepare the students for further education as well as for later professional and community life."[34] Thus, in addition to a focus on specific subjects, there is also an emphasis on Norwegian cultural heritage and values. Because Norway has an official state church, Evangelical-Lutheran, schools are permitted to bring Christian teachings into the classroom as a means of promoting shared values. Some feel, however, that this practice is inconsistent with promoting tolerance and intellectual freedom, especially in light of Norway's increasingly diverse population and varying religious beliefs. Others feel as long as particular beliefs are not forced on the students, teaching Christianity in the classroom should not be seen as a problem.

UNIVERSITY AND ADULT EDUCATION

Many educational opportunities exist for continuing education beyond high school. Norway has four universities offering bachelor through doctoral degrees. The University of Oslo is the oldest, largest, and most comprehensive of the universities. The other three universities were established after World War II, in Bergen, Trondheim, and Tromsø. The new universities offer a full range of subjects but also have specialty areas. Trondheim, for example, emphasizes technological fields, while Tromsø offers a program in Arctic studies. There are also six specialized colleges around the country, including a veterinary school, an agricultural college, a school of architecture, and a business school. Attendance is free, but admission is highly competitive.

Additionally there are over one hundred regional colleges that provide shorter programs of from one to three years in a broad range of fields, from nursing, to business administration, to social work, to foreign languages. The focus of these schools is upgrading the professional competence of people who live and work in the area served by the college. Because some are located in remote areas, an entire college may have only a few hundred students, and only ten colleges have more than a thousand. Many people view as admirable the government's attempt to make a college education available close to people's homes, but it is clear that quality of instruction and range of course offerings cannot always be maintained in these institutions. For this reason the regional colleges are considered the weakest link in Norway's educational system.

Adult education completes the educational picture in Norway and is meant to provide educational opportunities for those whose background would make attending an upper secondary school or a college inappropriate. Basic literacy, Norwegian as a Second Language, and some kinds of vocational training are among the adult education offerings. The opportunities are widespread, offered not only by the state but also by volunteer organizations, corporations, and other concerned groups.

WORK

Norwegians do their work in a variety of places. For many it is on the deck of a fishing boat. For others it is in a field of oats or a dairy barn. For still others it is behind the counter of a store, or seated at a desk in an office. Thus, it is impossible to generalize about where and when people work or what they do at work. Still, many scholars have written about the general attitudes of Norwegians towards work, and to a certain degree these attitudes apply whether one makes a living hauling in cod from the sea or managing a corporation in the city.

First, Norwegians expect to work hard. Work is an important part of their self-respect, and Norwegians set great store by such things as showing up on time and meeting deadlines. They do not tolerate a great deal of what they perceive as wasted time. This intolerance can be a bit disconcerting to foreigners doing business in Norway, because there will be no small talk to break the ice, and hardly even a greeting, before business is brought up.

On the other hand, according to writer Elizabeth Su-Dale, "Norwegians believe in the distinct separation of work and play."[35] Even people in highly responsible positions leave work promptly at the established quitting time. Meetings generally

COMMUTING, NORWEGIAN STYLE

"It is one thing to speak the same language and another thing to speak the same culture," claims American-born anthropologist Anne Cohen Kiel, a longtime resident of Oslo, in her essay "Confessions of An Angry Commuter," in *Continuity and Change: Aspects of Contemporary Norway.* Shortly after arriving in Oslo, she tried out her newly learned Norwegian on an elderly woman. "I smiled at her, nodded, and produced a *'God dag.'* Startled, the woman took a step in my direction, looked me over from top to toe and replied *'Jeg kjenner Dem ikke'* (I don't know you), and then she turned away." In a similar vein, Kiel reports that even after living in the same place for three years and commuting with the same neighbors every day, "we do not even nod in recognition of each other. On the contrary, we see each other and then quickly avoid eye contact." Generally Norwegians will not offer their seats to old people on buses, a situation which once prompted an advertising campaign designed to shame them into changing their perspective. "Here comes an old man," the posters on buses read. "Shall I pretend I don't see him?" Even in situations where everyone's safety would be enhanced by speaking to others on a crowded bus or tram, Norwegians will remain silent. Even if they spill coffee or accidentally trip someone, it is uncommon to say "excuse me."

Kiel explains that this reticence is probably due in part to Norwegians' keen desire for privacy. When she asked Norwegians about their behavior on public transportation, "quite a few said something to the effect that Norwegians are so afraid to attract attention to themselves that even in a potentially dangerous situation they clam up." They value their privacy and personal space to such a degree that they do not wish to change any situation into one in which they might be expected to carry on a conversation with a stranger. Hence they simply pretend that other people are not there. To Norwegians, this does not seem rude, because they feel other people wish to be left alone as well. What Americans might see as pleasantries or courtesy, a Norwegian would see in the opposite way, as an uncivilized violation of another person's boundaries, and as an unnecessary calling of attention to oneself. A "Hello," or even an "Excuse me," it seems, could ruin someone's day.

do not run late, and dawdlers in offices or stores will be reminded that it is time to leave. All this happens because Norwegians value highly their personal lives. They want to get home to their families and get started on their evening plans.

Although farmers and fishermen labor as the workload requires, employees in offices and stores have regular hours. Full-time work is forty hours over a five day period. Most offices open at 8 A.M. and close at 4 P.M., Monday through Friday, but adjustments are common. When an office or store is open more than eight hours, employers are usually flexible about which eight hours the employee works. Employers expect to make adjustments for those workers having children to get off to school, for example.

BENEFICIAL LABOR LAWS

In Norway, there are more laws protecting employees from overwork than in the United States. For example, anyone working more than forty hours in a week is legally entitled to 40 percent overtime pay. An employee has a legal right to a minimum of thirty-six hours of free time at one point during the week and must have at least ten hours between shifts. People whose jobs require weekend work must have at least one Sunday free every three weeks. Breastfeeding mothers have a right to work one hour less each day and may choose whether this benefit involves shorter overall hours or a longer break in the middle of the day.

Norway is also generous about vacation and sick leave. All workers are entitled to four weeks holiday per year even if they work less than full time. Employees older than sixty have five weeks a year. People have a legal right to take three of their vacation weeks in the summer. In addition, many offices also close for two weeks at Christmas. Rather than earning a specific number of sick days per year, people may use sick leave up to four times a year, with the numbers of days tied to the nature of the illness. For long illnesses, the employer pays the full salary for two weeks, then the government takes over responsibility. Parents may use up to ten days per year to care for a sick child.

Wages in Norway are fairly high overall, with the average salary hovering around $27,000 per year. One extra benefit of working in Norway is that employees get a holiday bonus. Holiday pay, or *feriepenger,* is a supplement of approximately 10 percent of the annual wage, paid in a tax-free lump sum to cover the additional expenses of holiday travel and activities. Norwegians appreciate *feriepenger,* but the taxes they pay on base wages are among the highest in Europe. Those taxes do pay for a very high level of service, however. Medical care, child care, education, pensions, unemployment insurance, and many community services are provided from tax revenues. Social security taxes, medical insurance premiums, and unemployment taxes are not extra deductions from wages, as they are in the United States. Instead, these charges are included in the general taxes paid. Income tax is graduated so that higher earners pay an even higher proportion, but the average income tax payment is approximately one third of a person's salary. There is also a "wealth tax"—paid on the value of possessions such as a house or car—as well as local, county, and state taxes. In addition, approximately 22 percent is added as sales tax to the cost of many items. Supplemental taxes on top of the 22 percent drive the prices of luxury goods like alcohol, cosmetics, and cigarettes even higher. Norwegians often complain that they pay and pay and pay. But they do receive many benefits they might otherwise have had to purchase separately.

LIFE AT HOME

One line in the Norwegian national anthem states clearly how Norwegians feel about the way they live: "Hytter og hus, men ingen borge," ("Hut or house, but no castles").[36] As in education and all other aspects of life, Norwegians frown upon deviations from the norm. No individual, it is felt, should be much poorer or much richer than another. Though obviously farmers living in remote regions are likely to lead more austere lives than professional people living in Oslo, the extremes of wealth and poverty seen in much of the rest of the world are lacking in Norway. Thus, certain generalizations can be made about the way typical Norwegians live.

The average Norwegian lives modestly, in a small but tidy and attractive home. Wherever possible, children have their

The average Norwegian family lives modestly and enjoys a peaceful home life; parents and children share mutual respect for each other and understand that family comes first.

NORWEGIAN CUISINE

The main meal for most Norwegians is *middag*, eaten at around 5 P.M., or a little earlier in rural areas. *Middag* is usually a one-course meal, consisting of meat or fish, potatoes, and a seasonal vegetable. It may also consist of some of Norway's favorite national dishes, such as fishballs in white sauce, meatballs in brown sauce, or various kinds of stew. *Middag* is a family meal, and most Norwegian families make a point of eating together at least this once every day.

Breakfast is also considered an important meal. A number of foods are put on the table, and people help themselves to whatever they want. Usually—in addition to bread, butter, and jam—plates of cold cuts such as ham and sausage will be served, as well as several kinds of cheese, eggs, and pickled herring. Lunch is similar, but may have shellfish, one or more hot dishes, and a dessert in addition. Workers and school children usually make sandwiches from the food put out at the breakfast table to take with them for lunch.

Two foods which seem a bit odd to outsiders but which are very popular in Norway are lutefisk and brown cheese, or *geitost*. Often served at Christmas, lutefisk is dried cod soaked in lye-water for several days until it is soft enough to press a finger through without resistance. The fish is then soaked in fresh water, preferably running water, for two more days to rinse out the lye, then boiled or poached. Gelatinous and translucent, lutefisk is definitely an acquired taste.

The color of peanut butter, *geitost* is a fairly soft cheese which is made in huge blocks from a mixture of goat's milk and cow's milk. In 1990, a radio station invited Norwegians to nominate the one object or trait that was most Norwegian. People nominated songs, objects such as knitted patterned mittens and the Hardanger fiddle, among other things. The winner was *geitost,* the brown cheese.

own rooms. Most houses make at least some provision for a play space, especially if there are not enough bedrooms for every child to have one for him or herself. This provision is important because people are indoors for long periods in the winter, and both adults and children need separate spaces for entertaining their friends. It is common for children to visit friends after school and in the evening. And adults who know each other very well may exchange visits from time to time—most adults, however, relish their private time at home in the evenings and on weekends, and socializing is fairly limited.

The emphasis in Norway is on mutual respect, and nowhere is this attitude more apparent than in the home. It is common for men to help around the house and take responsibility for the children, although studies indicate disagreement as to whether the men actually shoulder their full share of the burden. Norwegian men (and working women) tend to come straight home from work, seeing their family as far more important than mere after-work socializing with business acquaintances or personal friends. Likewise, Norwegian children are expected to put the family first. They have chores and are expected to show good manners and follow rules at home and elsewhere. In return, parents are expected to respect their children. Physical punishment in any form is against the law. According to Elizabeth Su-Dale, "Parents, teachers, or other adults who violate this law by smacking, hitting, or hurting a child, whether at home, outside, or in school, can be imprisoned."[37]

Recently, however, some breakdown in the generally mutually respectful adult-child relationship has been observed. Defiant and delinquent behavior in teenagers, particularly in school, is mounting, although it is still unusual. This change in behavior may be tied to an increase in the availability of street drugs, particularly in Oslo. A recent study in the Oslo area indicated that about 20 percent of the teenagers surveyed used hashish, having begun doing so at an average age of thirteen or fourteen. Though this percentage is still low compared to those of many other countries, Norwegians are alarmed. Much of Norwegian culture is tied to fitting in, and drugs are perceived as something that will alienate the young and tear at the overall social fabric. Likewise, drinking, though expensive, is a common form of entertainment among teens. Like parents everywhere, Norwegian mothers and fathers worry about the potential dangers and consequences of such behavior.

A Typical Weekend in Oslo

Observers of Norwegian life and customs often comment that regardless of where Norwegians live, they try to live as much as possible as if they lived in the countryside. During the week, Oslo parks are crowded with workers who have packed lunches so as to avoid crowded restaurants and be able to sit among the trees and birds. Evenings after dinner are often spent in some outdoor activity. In fact, many Oslo residents endure longer commutes than necessary in order to live far enough out of town to have a floodlit ski trail or a cycling or walking path nearby.

However, downtown does have its attractions as well, and it is on an Oslo weekend that the full range of Norwegian interests and activities may be observed. For many, Friday night is going-out night. Usually going out involves first returning home from work to eat and change clothes. Then, depending upon a person's age and the season, the individual might hang out in the town center with friends, do some bar-hopping, or perhaps just go to the movies.

Saturday is when most people take care of personal tasks. People may spend the morning shopping, then work around the house or garden in the afternoon. Many also spend part of the day watching sports on television. Saturday night is the most common night to have dinner with friends, at home or in a restaurant, followed by drinks at home.

Sunday morning some Norwegians go to church, but Sunday is best known as *tur* day (tour day). According to writer Anita Peltonen, "the *tur* is a walk or ski tour, and a formidable tradition. Depending on a person's age and the number of accompanying children, the *tur* can be anything from a one to six hour affair, [including] lunch in the forest. Some walks will include cafe stops in one of the 70-odd cabin lodges in the Nordmarka area of Oslo; if not, coffee and hot chocolate come along in a vacuum flask."[38]

In Norway, daily life is filled with the challenges of balancing demands of home, work, and school—just as elsewhere in the world. However, with its strong cultural emphasis on mutual respect, regardless of age, occupation, gender, or role—an emphasis demonstrated clearly in even the most routine daily activities—it seems apparent that Norway has a solid ethical and practical base on which to rely as it faces future challenges.

Arts and Entertainment

Norwegians do not spend every minute of their free time out of doors. Although their emphasis decidedly does lie in sports of all kinds, Norwegians also value the arts, and Norway abounds with bookstores, museums, festivals, and park sculptures. As in all things Norwegian, many of the most popular art forms are modest ones which ordinary people can do themselves, such as carving and painting wood, or weaving and embroidering textiles. Norway, however, has also produced some of the greatest achievements of recent centuries in the major art forms of music, drama, literature, and visual arts.

FOLK ARTS

Norwegians love to decorate the things which surround them. Blouses are trimmed with embroidered patterns, doors and doorways sport carved designs, and even furniture is painted with curving vines and bright flowers. This urge to decorate has its roots in the Viking era, when the prows of ships were carved with dragon heads and other figures. Ashore, the pillars and sometimes the exterior walls of houses were elaborately carved with mythological figures, scenes of battle, and other motifs. At the beginning of the Christian era in Norway, in the twelfth century, love of decoration was extended to church buildings. Not only are the portals, or entrances, to the churches elaborately carved with both pagan mythological figures and Christian symbols, but the churches themselves are fancifully constructed of pieces of wood and shingles in decorative designs.

Objects in everyday use in that era, and the interiors of homes, were decorated as well. Presumably the use of bright colors of paint to decorate chairs, cupboards, beds and tables,

Many shops in Norway still display traditional woodcarvings.

as well as bowls, plates, ladles and other house-wares, was a way of cutting through the dreary darkness of endless winter nights. Painting, carving, and doing other crafts were also ways to spend the long indoor hours before spring brought work to do outside and more chances to get away from home. Carving and wood painting—called *rosemaling,* or rose painting (although a rose design is not actually very common in the style)—often occur together in one piece. Because neither wood nor paint tend to last very long, genuinely old rosemaling and carving are rare and thus extremely precious. The traditions have been handed down, however, and more and more people have recently become interested in learning the old crafts.

TRADITIONAL CLOTHING

Love of decoration is also apparent in the traditional dress of Norway, the *bunad.* The word *bunad* is a general term for clothes, and thus there evolved dress-up bunads and everyday bunads, each in the unique style of one particular valley or small region. Today, the term *bunad* is reserved for the folk costumes brought out on national holidays and celebrations such as religious confirmations and weddings. Typically, a woman's *bunad* will consist of a wool skirt and a bodice or jacket, often of a contrasting material, worn over a blouse. The skirt and bodice are usually decorated with multicolored embroidered ribbon or a woven design. The contrast between solid colors and the small but bright geometric, animal, or flower designs of the trim give the overall costume a cheerful look. Sashes and beautiful purses—sometimes made from pieces of silver—and traditional shoes complete the outfit. Regional variations abound, including the addition of different styles of hats, shawls, and aprons. A man's *bunad* consists of pants which buckle below the knee, long socks, and a jacket and vest worn over a white shirt. The jacket and vest are often trimmed in a manner similar to the women's costumes.

The other typically Norwegian clothing is a brightly patterned knitwear. Norwegian sweaters, hats, scarves, and mittens are very tightly woven to keep out the cold, and the sweaters are characterized by elaborate geometric designs. These designs vary from region to region. The workmanship is very good, and intricately patterned hand knit sweaters sell in stores for the equivalent of several hundred dollars. Women (and sometimes men) knit through the long winter and find a profitable market for their wares during the tourist season when steamer passengers and other travelers stop in their villages.

In addition to articles of clothing and woodworking, Norway is also well known for its beautiful, Viking-inspired pewterware, as well as lace-trimmed and embroidered table linens, and glass products. The area around Lillehammer is particularly noted for factories producing beautiful multicolored glassware. Many of the textiles, however, come from the hands of individual weavers and needleworkers, who create brightly pattered table runners, embroidered wallhangings, and other items to decorate the home—and from seamstresses who incorporate lacework and embroidery into linen and cotton fabrics they purchase. The Sami also specialize in intricate carvings in bone.

These young Norwegians are wearing bunad, *folk costumes still worn on national holidays and for events such as confirmations and weddings.*

LITERATURE

As illustrated by the popularity of folk art forms today, everywhere one looks in Norway, there seems to be a strong continuity with the past. This linkage may in part be because Norwegian children grow up with a strong sense of their nation's mythology and history from their school studies. It may also in part stem from the fact that Norway is a nation of readers, and that Norwegian literature often retains close ties to tradition. A typical family of four is likely to spend well over two hundred dollars in books each year, and visit the local library on numerous occasions. It is difficult to determine how much of an influence reading habits have on Norwegian national pride, but clearly their knowledge of themselves plays a role in their desire to keep unique traditions alive.

To learn about their past, Norwegians can consult several ancient sources. Stories originating in the Old Norse period (750 A.D.–1350 A.D.) are still read, and *Heimskringla,* a classic history of Norse kings written in the early thirteenth century by Icelandic historian Snorri Sturluson is, according to author Elizabeth Su-Dale, "still a best seller in Norway."[39] Mythological tales and early sagas of powerful families survive from inscriptions in runes and have been translated and published. Sami legends are also now being written down and translated into Norwegian. Also, references to the Vikings and their exploits abound in histories written in other countries, most notably England. In one such account dating from about 900 A.D., a boastful Viking chieftain—Ottar, from Finnmark in the far north of Norway—told the English king about his life. The king's scribe wrote it all down, and this surviving document is the best single source about life and attitudes in the Viking era.

Throughout the centuries other writers of renown shaped literature in Norway, among them Petter Dass in the seventeenth century, Ludvig Holberg in the eighteenth century, and Hendrik Wergeland in the early nineteenth century. What is known as the Golden Age of Norwegian literature, however, did not begin until the second half of the nineteenth century, when in the words of writer Jim Hardy, "literature became the smithy where the nation's identity was forged."[40] In this period, both the Nobel Prize–winning author Bjørnstjerne Bjørnson and the dramatist poet Henrik Ibsen lived and worked. Bjørnson was a prominent theater director who

KRISTIN LAVRANSDATTER

Nobel Prize–winning novelist Sigrid Undset brought medieval Norway to life in her famous trilogy *Kristin Lavransdatter.* The work follows the life of a strong-willed girl in northern Norway, who grows up to face many challenges. In this scene, early in the first novel, the young Kristin sees her first stained glass, which has recently been installed in a church in Hamar:

"Come over here," [Brother Edvin] said, leading Kristin to the foot of the scaffolding. He climbed a ladder and rearranged several planks high above. Then he went back down and helped the child to ascend.

On the gray stone wall above her, Kristin saw strange, flickering specks of light, red as blood and yellow as ale, blue and brown and green. She wanted to look behind her, but the monk whispered, "Don't turn around." When they stood together high on the planks, he gently turned her around and Kristin saw a sight so glorious that it almost took her breath away.

Directly opposite her on the south wall of the nave stood a picture that glowed as if it had been made from nothing but glittering gemstones. The multicolored specks of light on the wall came from rays emanating from the picture itself; she and the monk were standing in the midst of its radiance. Her hands were red, as if she had dipped them in wine; the monk's face seemed to be completely gilded, and from his dark cowl the colors of the picture were dimly reflected. She gave him a questioning glance, but he merely nodded and smiled.

It was like standing at a great distance and looking into heaven. Behind a lattice of black lines she began to distinguish, little by little, the Lord Jesus himself, wearing the costliest red cloak; the Virgin Mary in robes as blue as the sky; and the holy men and maidens in gleaming yellow and green and violet attire. They stood beneath the arches and pillars of illuminated houses surrounded by intertwining branches and twigs with extraordinary, bright leaves.

The monk pulled her a little farther out toward the edge of the scaffold.

"Stand here," he whispered. "Then the light will fall on you from Christ's own cloak."

commissioned plays with themes celebrating Norway's past. Bjørnson's poem "Yes We Love This Land of Ours" is now the national anthem of Norway. Acclaimed as the greatest literary figure in Norway, Henrik Ibsen wrote plays such as *Hedda Gabler* and *A Doll's House,* which raise issues about gender roles and are praised today for their feminist perspective.

HENRIK IBSEN

Norway's greatest playwright, Henrik Ibsen, was born in 1826 in Skien, a small village in Telemark. His father had to declare bankruptcy when Henrik was ten, so he was sent to be a druggist's apprentice in an even smaller town, Grimstad. Ibsen felt humiliated and disgraced by his family's misfortune, and the themes of alienation, hypocrisy, and social repression which often show up in his work may have had their genesis in the thoughts he had as he worked in the pharmacy.

Ibsen finally escaped rural Norway, which he hated, and lived in both Bergen and Oslo for a while, working in theaters and writing both poetry and plays. He seemed to fail at everything he tried, and eventually he gave up on the idea of being successful at presenting plays in Norway concerned with real Norwegians and real Norwegian issues. He went abroad, spending the next twenty-seven years in Germany and Italy, and it is in those countries that he wrote his best known works.

The first of these was *Pillars of Society*, which attacks small-town attitudes. Later he wrote *Ghosts*, whose theme, the effects of syphilis, was considered scandalous. According to Jim Hardy, writing in *Insight Guide: Norway*, the London *Daily Telegraph* ranted that the play was "positively abominable . . . a dirty act done publicly, a [lavatory] with all its doors and windows open . . . gross . . . crapulous stuff." Ibsen's best known work, however, is *A Doll's House*. Its heroine, Nora, ends up making some foolish decisions when she tries to act independently of her husband, but she finds the courage to defend her right to make decisions, even poor ones, and ends up leaving her husband and family in order to have a life of her own.

Ibsen returned to Norway toward the end of his life and was treated as a hero of Norwegian nationalism. He died in 1906 in Oslo.

Now hailed as Norway's greatest literary figure, poet and playwright Henrik Ibsen (1828–1906) composed controversial works on the subjects of alienation, hypocrisy, and social repression.

Other great writers appeared around the turn of the century. Knut Hamsun is another Nobel Prize–winning author, whose works include *Hunger*, an 1890 novel about an alienated young man. *Hunger* shocked readers of its day and had a great influence on later novelists. Hamsun's reputation suffered when he supported Germany's Adolf Hitler in World War II, but people have recently begun rediscovering the merits of his work. Yet another Nobel Prize–winning author is Sigrid Undset, whose trilogy about a woman in medieval Norway, *Kristin Lavransdatter*, published between 1920 and 1927, is one of the great classics of Norwegian fiction.

Undset is just one example of the many fine women writers Norway has produced. Others from the nineteenth century include Camilla Collett, whose novel *The District Governor's Daughters*, published in 1854, chronicles the struggles of young women against their social conditioning. Amalie Skran's novel *Betrayed*, written a generation later, deals with the sexual attitudes of her time through a story about a young woman married to a sea captain much older than she.

Although his reputation suffered due to his support of Adolf Hitler in World War II, author Knut Hamsun (1859–1952) received the Nobel Prize for literature in 1920.

MODERN LITERATURE

According to author Elizabeth Su-Dale, "Norway enjoys a rich diversity in literature, not least owing to the official cultural policy. One thousand copies of most Norwegian books of fiction, poetry, and drama are purchased for distribution to libraries around the country. Many writers have also been granted a guaranteed annual income by the government."[41] As a result, many people, including a large number of women following in the tradition of Undset, have been able to make a career out of their skill as writers. Notable women writers of the last few decades are Sigrid Hoel and Cora Sandel. Sandel's trilogy—*Alberta and Freedom, Alberta Alone,* and *Alberta and Jacob*—chronicle, much as Undset's trilogy did earlier, the struggle of a young woman to thrive in an environment which seems to work against her.

More recently, a new generation of Norwegian women has burst onto the literary scene. Cecilie Løveid's novel *Sug*

This famous painting, Skrik, more commonly known as The Scream, *was created by Norwegian painter Edvard Munch (1863–1944). Approximately fifty versions of the painting exist.*

(Suck) shocked critics but gained her an international reputation for cutting-edge writing. The writers Live Køltzow and Kari Bøge focus on the contemporary lives and problems of women, using raw but highly expressive language. However the most famous Norwegian novelist today is a man, Jostein Gaardner, whose work *Sophie's World* is a history of philosophy interwoven with a fictional plot. Jules Brown and Phil Lee, writers of *Norway: The Rough Guide,* call it a "hugely popular novel that deserves all the praise heaped upon it," adding that it is "beautifully and gently written, with puffs of whimsy . . . and an engaging mystery story too."[42]

PAINTING AND SCULPTURE

In the visual arts, Norway has also produced several important figures. Preeminent among them is Edvard Munch, the highly original and eccentric creator of the famous painting *The Scream.* In *The Scream,* of which there are approximately fifty versions, a man stands on a bridge, his mouth and eyes open with alarm, while below him rushes a river and above him swirls a menacing, garishly colored sky. Munch's other most famous paintings include *The Vampire,* which depicts a woman bending over a slumped figure of a man. Her long, bright red hair streams over his head, suggesting that she has already bitten his neck and begun her feast.

In an entirely different style, but equally influential on Norwegian art, is landscape painter J. C. Dahl. His huge canvases of the Norwegian mountains and valleys are majestic and contributed a great deal to the growth of national pride in the late nineteenth century, when he was active as a painter. Dahl was also influential in creating the National Gallery in Oslo where many of his paintings hang today, along with works by his great contemporaries—such as husband and wife Christian and Osa Krohg, Harriet Backer, and Kitty Kielland. Christian Krohg is perhaps the best known, especially for his large painting of prostitutes lining up for medical checks while scornful society ladies look on. Important twentieth-century landscape artists

EDVARD MUNCH

"I was walking along a road with two friends. The sun set. I felt a tinge of melancholy. Suddenly the sky became blood red. I stopped and leaned against a railing feeling exhausted, and I looked at the flaming clouds that hung like blood and a sword over the blue black fjord and the city. My friends walked on. I stood there trembling with fright. And I felt a loud unending scream piercing nature."

Jules Brown and Phil Lee, in *Norway: The Rough Guide,* record these as the words which Edvard Munch (1863–1944) used to describe the experience that resulted in his most famous work, *Skrik,* or *The Scream.* It was painted in the 1890s, along with a number of equally emotionally charged works, such as *Virginia Creeper*—which depicts a house being consumed by a plant—and other paintings with such titles as *Anxiety* and *Despair.* The paintings and woodblock prints from this period are considered the core of his work, although his style changed several times during his career.

By the time Munch was in his early twenties, he was already experimenting with ways of showing emotions and inner feelings in his canvases and prints. His early work *The Sick Child* depicts his tortured childhood memories of his sister Sophie's death from tuberculosis. Always an emotionally fragile man, Munch had a nervous breakdown in 1908 from overwork, alcoholism, and unhappy love affairs. He retreated to a small village on the Oslofjord, where his

work came to reflect a tranquillity previously missing. Heavy drinking, however, and continued bouts of depression are reflected in his later pieces. Reputed in his youth to be the best-looking man in Norway, Munch, in *Self-Portrait by the Window,* one of his last paintings, in the words of Jules Brown and Phil Lee, appears as "a glum figure on the borderline of life and death, the strong red of his face and green of his clothing contrasted with the ice-white scene visible through the window."

Edvard Munch's heavy drinking and depression influenced many of his paintings, such as this self portrait.

Sculptor Gustav Vigeland's sculpture park, Vigelandsparken, *features a large number of statues, including the famous* Sinnetagen, *or* Angry Boy.

include Gladys Nilssen Raknerud and Thorbjørn Lie-Jørgensen. They join Arne Ekelund, Rolf Nesch, Sigurd Winge, Per Kleiva, Odd Nerdrum, and Jakob Weidemann as among the most highly regarded modern Norwegian artists.

Next to Edvard Munch, sculptor Gustav Vigeland is probably the best-known Norwegian artist. This notoriety is a bit ironic, since the two were bitter rivals as artists and as men, after they fell out over a mistress they shared. Vigeland's masterpiece is the Vigelandsparken, a sculpture park in Oslo. There, the visitor enters across a bridge lined with fifty-eight bronze figures of people of both sexes and all ages, including the famous tantrum-throwing *Sinnetagen,* or *Angry Boy.* The visitor next comes to a fountain with a series of twenty carved stone panels depicting the cycle of life. Further beyond, the visitor sees a fifty-five-foot-high spire, the *Monolitten,* or monolith, sculpted from one piece of granite. Upon a closer look, the viewer sees that the monolith consists of many intertwined human figures—121 in all. Together they constitute, in the words of Elizabeth Su-Dale, "a totem pole of figures clambering up, child upon man upon woman, interlinked in fate and destiny."[43] Below the monolith, arranged on the steps leading up to it, are thirty-six groups of granite figures engaged in different activities. The last of the sculptures in the park is the *Livshjulet,* or *Wheel of Life,* which writer Jim Hardy describes as "a continuum of human figures in a kind of airborne ring dance."[44]

Vigeland's sculptures are realistic depictions of people, and several other sculptors also work in that same vein. Most notable among them are Nils As and Bøge Berg. Another well-known Norwegian sculptor, Arnold Haugeland, has gone in a different direction and has become famous for his abstract works. These artists find Norway a good place to work in because of government support for art. According to Jim Hardy, "there are more twentieth century sculptures [and] statues per capita in Norway than in any other country in Europe."[45]

TROLLS AND GIANTS

Trolls and giants are perhaps the most prominent figures in Norwegian imagination, and they play the biggest role in stories about the origin of geological sites around the country. Trolls are said to live everywhere—in the woods, in the water, in caves under waterfalls. They can on occasion be helpful to humans, but for the most part they are malicious, stealing children, abducting young women, and otherwise making life difficult. They are small and misshapen but very powerful. Their two greatest weaknesses are that they cannot stand noise and that sunlight turns them to stone. As late as the 1700s Norwegians believed that the loud tolling of church bells was the best way to scare them off. Also all over Norway, people can point to evidence of rocks which they claim are actually trolls turned to stone, or evidence of damage done by mischievous trolls. Today people still claim to see trolls, although the typical sighting is more likely to be only toy figures on the shelves of tourist shops.

Giants are not only large but very strong. Some are helpful and kind, but others are cruel. All giants are reputed to be quite stupid and easily fooled. One of their favorite things to do is to pick up boulders or large chunks of the landscape, carry them someplace else and drop them. According to the earliest Norse myths, Ymir was a giant who was a descendant of the Frost Giants who lived in Jontuheim. Ymir was killed by Odin, the leading Norse god, and from Ymir's body the world was made.

Many Norwegian myths involve trolls and giants. The earliest Norse myths trace the creation of the world to Ymir, a giant whose body was used by the god Odin to make the world.

ARCHITECTURE

In the words of Elizabeth Su-Dale, "Norwegian architects to-day are international, yet there is still a quest for a national, uniquely Norwegian style."[46] For some this search has meant incorporating elements of traditional structures such as stave churches and Viking log houses into their architectural designs. For others the search has meant adapting what they perceive as Nordic simplicity to build beautiful but sleek and unfussy buildings which bring out the natural beauty of the materials used. Some manage to combine the two approaches, creating for example a roof turned up on an otherwise modern looking building, suggesting the tip of a ski or the prow of a Viking boat. A further example of this sort of design is the Hamar Olympic Hall, whose distinctive shape, resembling an overturned Viking ship, was built for the Lillehammer Olympic Games. The most renowned Norwegian architect in recent years is Sverre Fehn whose buildings are made of concrete, wood, and glass and which use light so

Built for the Lillehammer Olympic Games, Hamar Olympic Hall's architecture is suggestive of an overturned Viking ship.

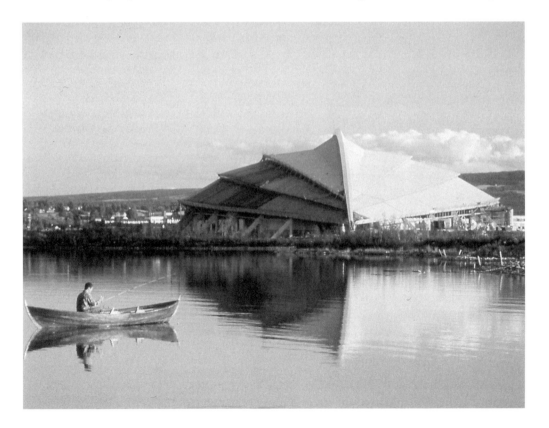

extensively that it becomes a fourth element of the building. In 1997 Fehn received the American Pritzker Architecture Prize, the equivalent of the Nobel Prize in his field.

MUSIC

On a level with Edvard Munch in art and Henrik Ibsen in literature is Edvard Grieg in music. Grieg's work was inspired, as was the work of other composers of the nineteenth century, by folk melodies and the unique sounds of the old instruments used to play them. One such instrument is the Hardanger fiddle, a violin-like instrument whose strings permit a much more complex array of sounds at one time than does a normal violin. This folk instrument was championed by Ole Bull, a Norwegian violinist widely reputed to rival Paganini for the title of best violinist ever. Grieg composed his most famous work, the *Peer Gynt Suite,* as music to accompany Henrik Ibsen's play *Peer Gynt.* An easygoing and charming man, Grieg was immensely popular on the Oslo concert scene in the 1860s and 1870s, and a fixture on international tours throughout his life. Grieg's greatest love, however, was his famous house at Troldhaugen, near Bergen, which is now a museum kept exactly the way it was when he died, down to the untidy jumble of sheet music scattered around the piano.

An instrument much like a violin, the Hardanger fiddle was played by such Norwegian musical talents as Ole Bull.

Music based on Norwegian folk tradition is still vibrant today, and the Hardanger fiddle so loved by Grieg and Bull can still be heard when traditional music is played. Much of that music performed today also involves folk dances such as the *halling,* which requires sufficient acrobatic skill for a male dancer to leap gracefully and kick a hat from the hand of a woman standing on a chair. It is traditional vocal music, however, for which Norway is best known. According to *World Music: The Rough Guide,* "Norway is unsurpassed in the Nordic countries for its tradition of vocal music, with many prominent singers,"[47] including the internationally praised vocalist and band leader Mari Boine.

Yet despite their rich folk traditions, Norwegian young people today favor the same kinds of music as do their counterparts

MARI BOINE

According to *World Music: The Rough Guide,* Sami singer Mari Boine's music "is dominated by her strong and urgent voice, plus a few carefully selected instruments from peoples all over the world," including the African drum which she often plays while she sings. Her musical style has evolved in part as a means of expressing her pride in being Sami. Until recently the Sami have been discouraged from maintaining their traditions, and *World Music: The Rough Guide* quotes Boine as saying in a recent interview, "Over the last ten years I've been fighting this feeling of being inferior to Norwegians or western people and my voice got stronger as I decided I wouldn't let anyone oppress me and that I have a value as a Sami."

Boine's high-energy music conveys more than ethnic pride, however. It is filled with messages about unity of people with each other and with the natural world. In her interview she says,

> Money is not important and power is not important. It's more your personality, the human being that is important. I used to think men oppressing women or governments oppressing people knew what they were doing and were just cynical. But then I realized that they often are unaware and are filled with fear. I feel I have to find my way to their hearts to let them know what they are doing. It's the only way to change things.

Lyrics such as these, quoted by *World Music: The Rough Guide* from her song "Gula Gula," show her convictions clearly:

Hear the voices of the foremothers

Hear

They ask you why you let the earth become polluted

Poisoned

Exhausted

They remind you where you come from

Do you hear?

Again they want to remind you

That the earth is our mother

If we take her life

We die with her.

around the world. Techno music is very popular, as are American oldies and songs on *Billboard*'s weekly top forty list. Local night clubs are dominated by DJs playing both new hits and old favorites, or by local bands who play either their own compositions or cover-versions of hits. Although teens feel somewhat isolated geographically and—like other Norwegians—eager to keep up with the latest trends from the United States and Europe, they are proud of their own culture and generally more than happy to remain where they are, partaking on their own terms of what the world has to offer.

6

FACING THE FUTURE

Pictures of little red houses on calm, blue-green fjords with magnificent mountains rising up behind them might lead to the impression that Norway is a land of great tranquillity, a place where the snow piled high outside the front door in the winter is likely to be the biggest problem a person might face. In many respects, it is true that Norway has managed to avoid or at least minimize some of the problems and stresses associated with life in much of the rest of Europe and the United States, but daily life still presents many challenges. Likewise, the nation's political, economic, and social future seems more cloudy and troubled than the serene images in photographs may suggest.

Norwegians are proud of the way in which their government's economic and social policies have ensured a decent standard of living for everyone. They are proud of their educational system, which provides opportunities for all young Norwegians to continue their education as long as they have the desire and the capacity to do so, and also provides for older Norwegians to return to school to upgrade skills and pursue their interests. Norwegians value their role as international diplomats. And Norwegians see their interest in the outdoors as a sign of their overall fitness and strength as a people. In fact, many Norwegians believe that the rest of the world could take a few lessons from them about how to live high-quality lives and how to run a country.

Still, Norwegians are also worried. Their deep seated desire for fairness and equality was easy to fulfill when the economy was booming, as it has been throughout the lifetime of most of today's population. However, falling revenues from North Sea oil and gas; depleted catches of herring, cod, and other fish; environmental stresses such as acid rain; new influxes of immigrants; increased use of social services by retired, aging, and immigrant residents; and other equally pressing issues are all putting Norway's idealism to the test.

The Welfare State

Norwegian idealism is shown in concern for other people and in the belief there is no weakness or shame in needing help. From the twelfth century, when "by law the king obliged all farmers, for a specified number of days, to provide housing and food for paupers passing by,"[48] Norwegians have understood that everyone needs help at times and that generosity is eventually repaid. Thus, support was widespread for the development of what economists now call the "Scandinavian welfare model"[49] in the years after World War II.

According to sociologists Kåre Hagen and Jon M. Hippe, the Norwegian welfare state "has been built on three basic principles, or pillars. The first is the universal insurance of every citizen against all major cases of income loss and sickness."[50] This principle means that each individual is guaranteed a pension, unemployment insurance, medical care, and paid sick leave. Norwegians do not earn these things through their employment but instead have them as basic rights of citizenship. According to Hagen and Hippe, "Unlike the systems found in other countries, there is no formal link between an individual's contribution and the rights accumulated."[51] Norwegians believe that everyone is entitled to have a decent standard of living and good medical care regardless of social or economic position, and regardless of work history.

The second basic principle is that when an individual cannot work, his or her income should remain as close as possible to what it was while the person was working. According to Hagen and Hippe, "The argument is that the involuntary interruption of paid work, be it temporary or permanent, should not imply any substantial decline in . . . standard of living."[52] Welfare is not just for the poor, nor does it have any stigma attached to it. All nonworking people, regardless of their former income or social status, are entitled to continue to live as much as possible as they had when they worked. The assumption is that people wish to work because it is an important part of a person's identity

ARE YOU SPEAKING NORWEGIAN OR NORWEGIAN?

One of the hottest issues in Norway today involves the language itself. There are actually two Norwegian languages, *bokmål* and *nynorsk* ("new" Norse), and the issue of whether both languages should be taught in school is causing divisiveness and resentment around the nation. The two languages evolved during the time of the combined kingdoms of Denmark and Norway, when Danish words replaced Norwegian ones to the point that the standard language had become almost like Danish spoken with a Norwegian accent. When all across Europe in the nineteenth century a sense of ethnic and national pride was growing, some Norwegians decided that it was time to rescue their language and return it to its Old Norse roots. The leader of this effort was Ivar Asen, a linguist who used his remarkable knowledge of languages to try to construct how Old Norse would probably have evolved if the Danish had never influenced it. The language, *nynorsk,* was enthusiastically put into use, particularly in the western fjord regions around Bergen, and in some of the inland central areas as well.

Today Norway is still divided into those who speak *nynorsk,* about 20 percent of the population, and those who speak *bokmål* as their primary language. This situation causes some problems, because the languages are different enough that they need to be studied separately in school. The issue is an emotionally charged one. To some people *nynorsk* is a purer and truer form of Norwegian, and should be taught. Others favoring *bokmål* argue that having two languages works against national unity, and that time spent learning two forms of Norwegian could be better spent other ways, and that the study of *nynorsk* should be dropped.

Today there are rules requiring that the government use each language some of the time, and in fact the printing on Norwegian money uses some *bokmål* and some *nynorsk.* Though many people hope that the two languages will naturally merge over time, according to Elizabeth Su-Dale, in *Culture Shock: Norway,* "the problem of which language to use has been one of the burning issues in the literary and political life of Norway."

and self-esteem, and that they will work when and if they can. They should not suffer because of a situation beyond their control. Unemployment and disability payments are always proportional to former income and are not allowed to fall below what a person needs to remain in his or her home and provide for self and family.

The third principle is that the government has responsibility for providing all key social services and for footing the bill for pensions, unemployment insurance, and disability payments. Health services are also generally free, as is tuition through the university level. However, the cost of these benefits is astronomical, and Norwegians are taxed at one of the highest levels in the world on their income and their purchases. The income tax rate is extremely high, ranging from approximately one-third to two-thirds of earnings; and other taxes, on purchases and possessions, are also very steep. Because the highest earners pay the most taxes, thus reducing the amount of money they have available to spend, there are fewer extremes of wealth and poverty in Norway, and more equality of income than in most other countries.

THE HIGH COST OF EQUAL TREATMENT

The social commitment at the heart of the Norwegian welfare state is a source of national pride but also of growing concern. More than half of all the money in government coffers goes to finance social services. Though people complain about taxes, they are not willing to give up anything their taxes buy. However, many Norwegians fear they may have no choice but to pay more and get less because costs are expected to mount in the near future. The population nearing retirement age is growing and the number of young wage earners has shrunk as a result of a generally declining birth rate, so in the coming decades there will be fewer people to tax—and more people drawing benefits.

However, the cost of social services is only part of the burden born by Norwegians for their commitment to a decent standard of living for everyone. Norway's welfare state stretches far deeper than social services. When Norway made the decision to support people living in remote rural areas, building roads, bridges, tunnels, schools, and hospitals was only half the challenge. The other half was to make the lives in those areas more financially stable and sound. In a country where only 3 percent of the land is suitable for growing crops, farmers find it difficult to make ends meet. In some countries marginally producing farmers are forced to abandon their land and seek employment in nearby cities, or else find themselves taken over by huge farming corporations. But Norway remains committed to the survival of the small, independent farm. This principle has required financial assistance to farmers. A small dairy farmer, for example, is not likely to have sufficient pasture or budget for feed to maintain a herd large enough to make a profit. Therefore, the government pays a certain sum in cash for every cow he keeps.

Because only 3 percent of the land in Norway is suited to producing crops, the government assists farmers financially to enable them to survive.

Other farmers are similarly assisted. Because Norway must import half its food due to its short growing season, the government subsidizes farmers to grow whatever they can, such as tomatoes in the far south, preferring by this means to keep money in the country rather than paying it to outside suppliers. Likewise, fishermen using small boats cannot compete financially with larger boats which can go out further and stay out longer in all kinds of weather, and thus are paid whatever their shortfall is, as an incentive to keep on fishing their traditional way. Similarly, the cost of providing schools, hospitals, and other services in outlying regions is far more expensive than in cities, but doing so is seen as an essential part of treating Norway's rural citizens equally. And because small farmers and fishermen do not make a lot of money, they contribute less in taxes, making the burden on city dwellers even higher.

In recent years, the much praised Norwegian solidarity and social commitment has been sorely tested by the size of the bill. The government controls key industries such as oil and gas production in the Norwegian Sea, and revenues from these sources have until recently enabled Norway to avoid confronting the fact that it does not generate enough money through taxes to have the kind of society it wants. As oil and gas revenues begin to fall, Norway will have to make some difficult decisions. Already, people are discovering that their needs will no longer be fully met by the government. Though tuition is still free at universities, students must take out loans to pay for housing and other expenses. Hospitalization is still free, but dental care is not. Waits for openings in child care centers are so long that many people give up and hire private nannies.

As services shrink, the tax burden seems more oppressive. People feel they have paid their taxes for things they are not getting, and see their remaining income dwindle as a result of additional, out-of-pocket payments for services the government used to provide. Thus, in Norway during the past decade, according to historian Rolf Danielsen, "the problems of the welfare state are . . . apparent to all."[53] Redistributing money by taking a large percentage from everyone and giving it back where it is needed raises questions as to "whether the redistributive process has gone too far; whether the welfare arrangements really serve their purpose; and whether society *ought* to keep all of them, or, indeed, *can* do so."[54]

IMMIGRATION

Further complicating Norwegians' feelings toward the welfare state is the influx of immigrants in recent years. How much of a problem immigrants really pose to Norway's social structure is a matter for debate. Their increase is steady and likely to continue, but their overall numbers are still small, comprising less than 5 percent of the population. The issue is not, for many Norwegians, the increase in numbers but, rather, who the new immigrants are. In the past, most non-Norwegians living in Norway were fellow Scandinavians. In 1976, only 16 percent of the immigrants were from Asia, Africa, or South America. In 1990 the figure had risen to 41 percent. Though Danes form the largest immigrant group, there are now as many Pakistanis as there are Swedes living in Norway. Other sizable groups include Vietnamese, Iranians, Sri Lankans, Turks, and Chileans, as well as small numbers of immigrants from Africa.

Norway prides itself on its open-mindedness toward other cultures, and it has indeed been one of the great world powers in terms of foreign aid and development projects in Africa and elsewhere. However, non-European foreigners in Norway are not always treated as well as other immigrants. According to anthropologist Litt Woon Long, "Accusations of racism in particular seem to cause Norwegians much discomfort and embarrassment. These accusations are at odds with their self-image of being tolerant, moral, and righteous members of the international community."[55] Still, immigration was not seen as a problem until recently, when some people, for whatever reasons, appear to want to fan concern about it into a crisis.

According to Litt Woon Long, "Partly, this uncomfortable mood is the result of a general lack of knowledge of basic facts and figures."[56] For example, crimes committed by immigrants are quickly interpreted as trends, and the drains on services by immigrants are often grossly overstated. Many Norwegians feel that the immigrants themselves have not done enough to become "Norwegian" as quickly as possible, thus creating strains in a country used to a great deal of cultural homogeneity. Long adds that "not unexpectedly, the media has [contributed] to perpetuating this simple and polarized mode of approaching the complex issues"[57] of immigration.

There are some real issues at stake if immigration continues along its present lines. Norway makes no distinction between citizens and noncitizens when it comes to such things as schooling and medical care. But recent immigrants have tended to be poorer, less educated, and less skilled than earlier immigrants, thus creating more of a drain on social services. A non-Norwegian speaking child is more expensive to educate because the Norwegian way is to provide whatever supplemental help is needed rather than remove the child to special classes or hold him or her back. Also, when young adults immigrate, as is increasingly the case in Norway, they soon start families and then require health care for their children as well. Immigrants use services they have not contributed to funding, causing resentment.

Norwegians divide into three groups over the issue of services to immigrants. The first group believes that the Norwegian people should do whatever it takes to help immigrants fit in and become economically successful as quickly as possible. If doing so involves special programs and services, this group feels such items should be provided. The second group believes that immigrants should receive as much as—but no more than—other Norwegians. The third group feels immigrants are entitled to less. This group feels that, in the words of Long, immigrants should "stand at the end of the queue for jobs, housing, etc. Surely, they argue, it is not fair that immigrants (who 'have not made any contribution to society') are entitled to goods and services which they themselves have difficulty in obtaining."[58] How Norwegians will resolve these conflicts remains to be seen, but it is unlikely that Norway will put aside its basic commitment to social equality and allow a permanently poor underclass of immigrants to evolve. If, however, the price of treating immigrants on the same basis as ethnic Norwegians creates a ferment of negative feeling, especially in financially uncertain times, the solidarity that has characterized Norway's past will inevitably be damaged.

THE ENVIRONMENT
Another complex issue of concern for Norwegians is the environment. Few countries have so much at stake in keeping

WHERE HAVE ALL THE PUFFINS GONE?

Overfishing of herring in recent years has produced problems up the food chain. One prime example is the decline in the puffin population. Puffins, birds beloved for their bright orange beaks, slightly comical expressions, and behavior, feed on juvenile herring, called "fry," which drift north along the Arctic coast. Puffins float on the ocean and dive down to catch the fish in sharp, curved beaks. In recent years, however, there have not been enough fry to feed new puffin offspring, and the birds have been breeding successfully only once every four years. This limitation has resulted in a 60 percent reduction in puffin numbers since 1979. Even in the Lofoten Islands, once a prime breeding ground, puffins are now infrequently seen.

Other birds such as the guillemot have been similarly affected by overfishing. Additional hazards introduced by humans—such as oil spills and other forms of water pollution, and death by drowning in fishermen's nets—have also taken their toll on puffin, guillemot, and other bird species.

The puffin population in Norway has dropped 60 percent due to the over-fishing of herring, their main source of food.

their environment unpolluted, for Norway's economy still depends heavily on fishing and timber, and the nation must be able to keep its small amount of arable land in production. The recent nuclear accident at Chernobyl, in Ukraine, was in many ways a wake-up call. The reindeer herds of the

Sami were devastated by radioactive fallout which poisoned the lichen on which they live and rendered their meat worthless for sale. And in June 2000, a Norwegian Sea oil rig broke loose in a violent storm, creating concerns about the potential for oil spills.

Even one such spill could ruin Norwegian fishing, which is already in a steep decline. Kjetil Hindar, a researcher at the Norwegian Institute for Nature Research in Trondheim, explains that "during the last 20 years the coastal ecosystem has gone through dramatic changes."[59] Cod and capelin, two important fish species, have been particularly affected. Fewer fish are available to catch, and human competition with whales and other ocean predators for the remaining stock creates problems for the survival of all species which depend on cod and other fish to survive. Salmon fisheries are common sights near fishing villages, where people raise fish inside enclosures until they are marketable size. Problems arise, however, when salmon escape—a common occurrence—because the salmon in captivity often have parasites and diseases which kill the wild salmon they come in contact with. According to Kjetil Hindar,

> it is evident that large scale culture of Atlantic salmon, or of any other fish species, must be better regulated with respect to containment and disease control, so that aquaculture can be developed without compromising the ecological and genetic integrity of the wild source population.[60]

Also at risk are Norway's forests. One kind of damage to them is caused by poor logging practices. Although new trees have been planted in clear-cut areas, this remedy is not altogether effective. Hindar points out, "dense spruce forest stocked by even-aged trees results in poor [growth] from worsened light conditions and competition."[61] Thus, trees planted for later harvest are not as healthy as they might be. Another broader problem, however, is that many animal and plant species depend on old forest, with its tangled mix of life. When trees are clear-cut, lichens and undergrowth are destroyed as well, threatening many species, such as wild grouse, which rely on them for food and protection. Another threat to forests

CREATING WOMEN LEADERS

According to Elizabeth Su-Dale in *Culture Shock: Norway,*

> The high proportion of female representation in politics did not happen by accident. Persistent and systematic efforts by women in the women's movement, in the political parties, and in public administration have been rewarded by enhanced female participation in all sectors of Norwegian life.

In 1965, there were only twelve women in the Storting, the Norwegian parliament, but now they hold over one third of the 165 seats. A woman has been president of the Storting; a woman has been prime minister; and women have headed various national political parties in Norway.

Assisting women in gaining greater political power is the quota system in most Norwegian parties. In 1973 the Liberal and Socialist Parties decided to take steps in their recruitment and election processes to ensure that women would comprise between 40 and 60 percent of their leaders at all levels, from local communities on up to the Storting itself. The Norwegian Labor Party extended this principle to membership in the prime minister's cabinet under Gro Harlem Brundtland. In the job market, equal rights legislation requires employers to take steps toward promoting women to high management positions. The law states that if women are underrepresented in the management of an organization, a woman must be chosen for a position if her qualifications are equal to the male candidates.

Equality is still far from being achieved, however. For example, there are approximately 450 male but only 30 female mayors of towns and cities. Also, in many fields requiring scientific, economic, or technical skills, men still hold most of the high positions because fewer women choose careers in those fields. Still, Norway serves as a good example of what can be accomplished when developing and using women's potential is a national priority.

is environmental pollution, most specifically acid rain. According to Hindar, "during one generation ten times more acid has been measured in the southernmost part of Norway,"[62] much of it drifting north from the industrial

cities of Europe. Norwegian plant life has little ability to
resist acid rain because the shallow soil in many locations
makes weakening of roots quickly fatal.

Norwegians, with their love of the outdoors, have been
sensitive to the need for taking steps to preserve the environment. Today, large national parks and other wilderness
areas are designated for the protection of specific habitats.
Reindeer still roam wild as a result of these efforts, and
species extinct or endangered in other places, such as the
wolf and musk ox, still live in Norway. Whaling has been
banned for all endangered species, and severely curtailed for
other species. Norwegians need to live, however, and their
occupations, such as fishing and forestry, inevitably put
stresses on other life forms. Sustaining the diversity and the
abundance of this beautiful land will be one of the challenges facing Norway in the new century.

ISOLATION OR INCLUSION?

Another issue on the minds of Norwegians today is how to
balance their hard-won independence with the growing
trend to treat all Europe as one economic region. This trend is
best illustrated by the emergence of the European Union,
which has introduced a single currency, the Euro, in place of
the national currencies of its members, and which has
dropped all barriers to trade within the Union. Norway has
declined to join, making it one of the very few European nations to do so. Although the Norwegian parliament, the Storting, strongly favored joining the Union, the proposal to join
was defeated by a thin margin in a national referendum. The
outcome was clearly the result of a negative attitude toward
the Union by residents of Norway's northern regions. Such
concerns were well-founded, because joining the Union
would have required changes in the tax structure and the subsidies paid to those northerners who could not make a living
on their own.

In general, Norway has joined organizations with other
nations only if it has seen a clear possible negative impact in
failing to do so. A shared border with the Soviet Union after
World War II was incentive enough for Norway to join the
United States and other nations in the North American
Treaty Organization (NATO), to insure that the Soviets would
not encroach on Norwegian territory. But after hundreds of

years of subjugation to Sweden and Denmark and a recent taste of loss of freedom under the Nazis, Norwegians generally think it is a better idea to be on their own. Although the issue is one likely to be revisited, Norway does not feel that the favored trade status it would gain by joining the European Union is worth giving up any control over its own destiny.

From the time of the Vikings, Norway has never looked only in one direction while charting its future. Today Norway's economic outlook is global. Its gaze is directed as strongly across the Atlantic towards the United States as to southern neighbors in Europe, and Norway does not fear going its way alone outside the European Union. If Norway later joins, it will do so only when that decision is in the best interests of all Norwegians. Such concern for the health and strength of the nation as a whole—as well as for every individual in it—is typical of Norway. This attitude toward life can perhaps be said to resemble the tracks left by a single pair of skis across a white meadow, tracks which, as they join those of other skiers grow into a web of connections that embraces everyone and everything.

Facts About Norway

Land

Borders: Finland (729 km), Sweden (1619 km), Russia (167 km)

Area: 324,220 square km (approximately the size of New Mexico)

Land: 307,860 square km

Water: 16,360 square km

Coastline: 21,925 km

Climate: temperate along coast, colder in winter in interior, rainy year-round on west coast

Terrain: glaciated, high plateaus, mountains, valleys, Arctic tundra in north, fjords along coast

Highest elevation: Glittertinden 2,472 km

Natural resources: fish, timber, petroleum, copper, natural gas, pyrites, nickel, iron ore, zinc, lead, hydropower

Land use: arable land, 3 percent; forests/woodlands, 27 percent; other, 70 percent

People

Population: 4,438,547 (July 1999 estimate); age 0–14, 20 percent; age 15–64, 65 percent; over 65, 15 percent

Population growth rate: 0.4 percent

Birth rate: 12.54 births per one thousand population

Death rate: 10.12 deaths per one thousand population

Infant mortality rate: 4.96 deaths per one thousand live births

Life expectancy at birth: 78.36 years; men, 75.55 years; women, 81.35 years

Total fertility rate: 1.77 childen born/woman

Religions: Evangelical Lutheran, 87.8 percent (state church); other protestant/Catholic, 3.8 percent; none/unknown/other, 8.4%

105

Literacy rate (definition: age fifteen and over who can read and write):
99 percent

GOVERNMENT

Country name in English: Norway, or Kingdom of Norway

Country name in Norwegian: Norge, or Kongeriket Norge

Government type: constitutional monarchy

Capital: Oslo

Administrative divisions: nineteen provinces

Independence: October 26, 1905, from Sweden; celebrated May 17
(Constitution Day)

Executive branch: chief of state, King Harald V; heir apparent, Crown
Prince Håkon Magnus (born 1973)

Head of Government: Prime Minister Kjell Magne Bondevik (since
1997), appointed by monarch with approval of Storting (parliament)

Cabinet: appointed by the monarch with approval of Storting

Elections: last held, September 15, 1997; next scheduled, September
2001

Flag description: red with a sideways blue cross outlined in white

ECONOMY

Gross domestic product (GDP): $109 billion

GDP real growth rate (1998): 2.4 percent, expected to drop to 1 percent in 2000

Per capita income: $24,700

Inflation rate: 2.3 percent

Labor force: 2.3 million

Labor force by occupation: services, 71 percent; industry, 23 percent;
agriculture, forestry, fishing, 6 percent

Unemployment rate: 2.6 percent

Budget: revenues, $48.6 billion; expenditures, $53 billion

Industries: petroleum and gas, food processing (primarily fish), ship-
building, pulp and paper products, metals, chemicals, timber,
mining, textiles, fishing

Agricultural products: oats, grains, beef, milk, fish

Exports ($39.8 billion): petroleum and petroleum products, machinery and equipment, metal, chemicals, fish

Imports ($37.1 billion): machinery and equipment, chemicals, metals, foodstuffs

Debt (external):   none

Currency: Norwegian krone

NOTES

CHAPTER 1: A RUGGED LAND AND PEOPLE

1. Robert Spark, "The Far North," in *Insight Guide: Norway.* New York: Langenscheidt Publishers, 1999, pp. 226–27.

2. Jules Brown and Phil Lee, *Norway: The Rough Guide.* London: Penguin Books, 1997, p. 224.

3. Spark, "The Far North," p. 332.

4. Quoted in Brown and Lee, *Norway: The Rough Guide,* p. 264.

5. Robert Spark, "Telemark and the South," in *Insight Guide: Norway,* p. 209.

6. Robert Spark, "Peak and Plateau," in *Insight Guide: Norway,* p. 193.

CHAPTER 2: THE LAND OF THE VIKINGS

7. Brown and Lee, *Norway: The Rough Guide,* p. 277.

8. Rowlinson Carter, "Beginnings," in *Insight Guide: Norway.* New York: Langenscheidt Publishers, 1999, p. 21.

9. Brown and Lee, *Norway: The Rough Guide,* p. 278.

10. Brown and Lee, *Norway: The Rough Guide,* p. 278.

11. Carter, "Beginnings," p. 22.

12. Carter, "Beginnings," p. 26.

13. Carter, "Beginnings," p. 24.

14. Knut Herne, "Land of the Norsemen," in *Norway: A History from the Vikings to Our Own Time,* Rolf Danielsen, et al., eds. Stockholm: Scandinavian University Press, 1995, p. 31.

15. Herne, "Land of the Norsemen," p. 31.

16. Herne, "Land of the Norsemen," p. 25.

17. Herne, "Land of the Norsemen," p. 25.

18. Herne, "Land of the Norsemen," p. 25.

19. Brown and Lee, *Norway: The Rough Guide,* p. 281.

CHAPTER 3: A COUNTRY LOST AND REGAINED

20. Brown and Lee, *Norway: The Rough Guide*, p. 283.

21. Quoted in Rowlinson Carter, "The 400 Year Sleep," *Insight Guide: Norway*, pp. 37–38.

22. Knut Helle, "The Political System of the Late Middle Ages," *Norway: A History from the Vikings to Our Own Time*, Rolf Danielson et al., eds. Translated by Michael Drake. Stockholm: Scandinavian University Press, 1995, p. 119.

23. Rowlinson Carter, "An Independent, Modern Country," *Insight Guide: Norway*, p. 50.

24. Carter, "An Independent, Modern Country," p. 51.

25. Carter, "An Independent, Modern Country," p. 56.

CHAPTER 4: NORWEGIANS AT WORK AND PLAY

26. Michael Brady, "Sporting Passions," *Insight Guide: Norway*, p. 110.

27. Brady, "Sporting Passions," p. 72.

28. Brady, "Sporting Passions," p. 107.

29. Brady, "Sporting Passions," p. 107.

30. Quoted in Barbara Øvstedal, *Norway*. New York: Hastings House, n.d., p. 26.

31. Elizabeth Su-Dale, *Culture Shock: Norway*. Portland, OR: Graphic Arts Center Publishing Co., 1995, pp. 153–54.

32. Su-Dale, *Culture Shock: Norway*, p. 152.

33. Oddvar Vormeland, "Education in Norway," in *Continuity and Change: Aspects of Contemporary Norway*, Anne Cohen Kiel, ed. Oslo: Scandinavian University Press, 1993, p. 212.

34. Vormeland, "Education in Norway," p. 214.

35. Su-Dale, *Culture Shock: Norway*, p. 191.

36. Quoted in Thomas Hylland Eriksen, "Being Norwegian in a Shrinking World," in *Continuity and Change: Aspects of Contemporary Norway*, p. 21.

37. Su-Dale, *Culture Shock: Norway*, p. 166.

38. Anita Peltonen, "Oslo," *Insight Guide: Norway*, p. 164.

CHAPTER 5: ARTS AND ENTERTAINMENT

39. Su-Dale, *Culture Shock: Norway*, p. 173.

40. Jim Hardy, "Tradition, Not Haute Couture," *Insight Guide: Norway*, p. 124.

41. Su-Dale, *Culture Shock: Norway,* p. 174.

42. Brown and Lee, *Norway: The Rough Guide,* p. 299.

43. Su-Dale, *Culture Shock: Norway,* p. 187.

44. Hardy, "Tradition, Not Haute Couture," p. 161.

45. Hardy, "Tradition, Not Haute Couture," p. 126.

46. Su-Dale, *Culture Shock: Norway,* p. 185.

47. Simon Broughton et al., *World Music: The Rough Guide.* London: Rough Guides, Ltd., 1994, p. 50.

CHAPTER 6: FACING THE FUTURE

48. Kåre Hagen and Jon M. Hippe, "The Norwegian Welfare State: From Post-War Consensus to Future Conflicts," in *Continuity and Change: Aspects of Contemporary Norway,* p. 86.

49. Anne Cohen Kiel, ed., *Continuity and Change: Aspects of Contemporary Norway,* p. 85.

50. Hagen and Hippe, "The Norwegian Welfare State: From Post-War Consensus to Future Conflicts," p. 86.

51. Hagen and Hippe, "The Norwegian Welfare State: From Post-War Consensus to Future Conflicts," p. 87.

52. Hagen and Hippe, "The Norwegian Welfare State: From Post-War Consensus to Future Conflicts," p. 87.

53. Danielsen, et al., *Norway: A History from the Vikings to Our Own Times,* p. 449.

54. Danielsen, et. al., *Norway: A History from the Vikings to Our Own Times,* p. 449.

55. Litt Woon Long, "Recent Immigration to Norway," in *Continuity and Change: Aspects of Contemporary Norway,* p. 186.

56. Long, "Recent Immigration to Norway," p. 186.

57. Long, "Recent Immigration to Norway," p. 186.

58. Long, "Recent Immigration to Norway," pp. 186–87.

59. Kjetil Hindar, "Nature and Conservation of Natural Resources," *in Continuity and Change: Aspects of Contemporary Norway,* p. 224.

60. Hindar, "Nature and Conservation of Natural Resources," p. 225.

61. Hindar, "Nature and Conservation of Natural Resources," p. 227.

62. Hindar, "Nature and Conservation of Natural Resources," p. 228.

CHRONOLOGY

3000 B.C.
Battle-Ax and Boat-Ax people establish first known permanent communities.

200 A.D.
Runes used to write language.

c. 600–699
Boats capable of long ocean voyages in use by Vikings.

793
Viking sack of Lindesfarne monastery in England.

857
First Viking sack of Paris. Two further sacks followed in 861 and 885.

c. 870
Beginning of Viking settlement of Iceland.

c. 880–931
Reign of Harald Hårfagri, first to rule a unified Norway. First records of parliamentary assembly, or *ting*.

c. 931–933
Reign of Eirik Bloodax.

c. 959–974
Reign of Harald Greycloak Erickson.

995–999
Reign of Olav Tryggvason.

1015–1028
Reign of Olav Haraldsson, later canonized as Saint Olav.

1028–1035
Reign of King Canute.

1030
Olav Haraldsson killed at Battle of Stiklestad.

1046–1066
Reign of Harald Hardråda, the last Viking king.

1349–50
Black Death kills as much as half the population.

1388–1412
Margareta is effective ruler in Scandinavia.

1397
Kalmar Union joins Norway, Denmark, and Sweden under one monarch, Erik of Pomerania.

1439
Erik of Pomerania dethroned.

1450
Danish and Norwegian union replaces Kalmar Union, with Christian of Oldenburg as king.

1468
Christian I gives away Norwegian territory in Shetland and Orkney Islands, indicating lack of respect for Norway's sovereignty.

1534–1559
Christian III reigns as king of Denmark and Norway.

1536
Christian III declares Norway to be a province of Denmark. Protestant Reformation begins in Norway.

1624
Oslo burns; rebuilt under name Christiania.

1807–14
Napoleonic Wars.

1814
In the Treaty of Kiel, Denmark loses Norway to Sweden at end of Napoleonic Wars. Christian Frederik attempts to seize crown, calling assembly which writes Norwegian constitution.

1818–1844
Reign of King Karl XIV Johan.

1905
Norway achieves independence from Sweden.

1940–1945
German occupation of Norway.

1947–53
Period of debate over future economic and social structure of Norway.

1949
Norway joins NATO.

1972
Norwegians vote against membership in European Economic Community (EEC).

1991
King Harald V, the present monarch, assumes throne.

1994
Norway votes down membership in European Union (EU).

GLOSSARY

arable: Suitable for farming.

bokmål: The dominant form of written and spoken Norwegian today.

bunad: The traditional folk costume of Norway.

coalition: A group of different political parties who come together to form a large enough voting bloc to control the government of a country.

ecosystem: Animal and plant species living in the same environment, whose survival is tied to functioning together as a unit.

fjord: An inlet of sea water between cliffs or steep slopes. If there is an outlet on the other side giving passage all the way though, it is called a strait rather than a fjord.

hytte: A cottage or hut in a natural setting used as a getaway by Norwegian families.

maritime: Having to do with the ocean.

nynorsk: A form of Norwegian invented in the nineteenth century as an expression of national pride, currently the first language of 20 percent of Norwegians.

province: An administrative division of a country.

puppet government: A government controlled by another outside power which "pulls the strings."

quisling: A traitor, from Vidkun Quisling, a Norwegian Nazi.

rosemaling: A traditional Norwegian form of decorative painting on wooden walls and furniture.

rune: A form of writing using only straight lines, which can be more easily carved into rock.

sabotage: An act to destroy or undermine efforts of an enemy. From the French *sabot,* or wooden shoe; the term refers to throwing a shoe into machinery to break it.

saboteur: A person involved in sabotage.

scorched earth policy: A military practice of burning villages and crops when retreating.

stipend: An amount of money paid to defray costs of a service rendered.

Storting: The Norwegian parliament.

subsidy: An amount paid by a government to make something profitable to produce or affordable to buy.

ting,* or *thing: A Norwegian medieval general assembly in which all free men could participate. *Lagting* and *Storting* are derived from *ting.*

Suggestions for Further Reading

Books

Peter Christian Asbjrnsen, ed., *East o' the Sun and West o' the Moon*. Minneola, NY: Dover Publications, 1970. A collection of fifty-nine Norwegian folk tales.

Hans Frederik Dahl, *Quisling: A Study in Treachery*. Cambridge: Cambridge University Press, 1999. Abridged version, translated by Anne Marie Stanton-Ife, of a classic study of Norwegian Nazi Vidkun Quisling.

Belinda Drabble and Michael Brady, *Living in Norway*. Oslo: Palamedes Press, 1999. First published in 1988, this revised edition provides thorough, up-to-date information about all aspects of life in Norway today.

Knut Haukelid, *Skis Against the Atom: The Exciting First Hand Account of Heroism and Daring Sabotage During the Nazi Occupation of Norway*. Minot, ND: North American Heritage Press, 1989. Memoir by one of Norway's most decorated military heroes of his experiences as one of the saboteurs at Telemark.

Hanna Aasvik Helmersen, *War and Innocence: A Young Girl's Life in Occupied Norway*. Seattle: Hara Publishing Group, 2000. Recently published memoir of the World War II years.

Elisabeth Holte, *Living in Norway*. New York: Abbeville Press, 1993. Beautiful photographs with a good accompanying text.

Lise Lurge-Larsen, *The Troll with No Heart in His Body*. New York: Houghton-Mifflin, 1999. Beautifully illustrated with woodcuts by Betsy Bowen, this collection of troll stories, including "The Three Billy Goats Gruff," is authored by a woman known in Minnesota as the Troll Lady.

Marie McSwigan, *Snow Treasure.* New York: Scholastic Press, 1997. Reissue of a popular novel about children in occupied Norway who smuggle 9 million dollars past the Nazis.

Mette Newth, *The Dark Light.* New York: Farrar, Strauss and Giroux, 1998. Translated by Faith Ingwersen, this grimly realistic novel has as its heroine a thirteen-year-old girl with leprosy living in a hospital in Bergen, and has as its theme the need to find goodness and positive meaning in the worst of situations.

Ingrid Semmingsen, *Norway to America: A History of the Migration.* Minneapolis: University of Minnesota Press, 1980. Translated by Einar Haugen, this book describes the immigration of Norwegians to the United States.

David M. Wilson, ed., *The Northern World: The History and Heritage of Northern Europe, AD 400–1100.* New York: Harry Abrams Publishers, 1980. Thorough introduction to all of the countries in northern Europe, including Norway, with many maps and illustrations.

Robert Wulf, *Norway: Welcome to the 1994 Olympic Games.* Hong Kong: Everbest Printing Company, 1994. Created for the Lillehammer Olympics, this book contains many beautiful photographs of Norway, as well as a good text about the various regions and traditions of the country.

WEBSITES

Digital City: Oslo (home.digitalcity.com/oslo/webguide). Good source of information about daily life and special events in Oslo.

The Nordic Pages (www.markovitz.com/nordic/norway. shtml). Good information in easy to use format, about culture, history, government, and other topics of interest, as well as links to newspapers, museums, and other sites.

WORKS CONSULTED

BOOKS

Simon Broughton and others, eds., *World Music: The Rough Guide.* London: Rough Guides, Ltd., 1994. Essential source for information about musical traditions and modern trends around the world, including Norway.

Jules Brown and Phil Lee, *Norway: The Rough Guide.* London: Rough Guides, Ltd., 1997. One in an excellent series of travel guides. Although the majority of the text contains information about sights of interest to visitors, it is also packed with well researched information about history, customs, and other things of interest.

Rolf Danielsen, et al., ed., *Norway: A History from the Vikings to Our Own Time.* Translated by Michael Drake. Stockholm: Scandinavian University Press, 1995. A thorough work by a number of noted historians from the University of Bergen. This volume was originally intended as the textbook accompanying a telecourse offered through the university.

David Howarth, *We Die Alone: A WWII Epic of Escape and Endurance.* New York: Macmillan, 1955. New edition, New York: Lyons Press, 1999. Chronicles the failed mission of a group of Norwegian saboteurs sent from Britain. The only survivor, Jan Baalsrud, survived for months under impossible odds before making it to safety in Sweden. Howarth's book is based on interviews with Baalsrud, those who helped him, and other authoritative sources.

Insight Guide: Norway. New York: Langenscheidt Publishers, 1999. The best single source for visitors and others interested in Norway. The outstanding photography and interesting sidebars complement a well researched text. The volume includes extensive chapters on history, lifestyles, and culture.

Anne Cohen Kiel, ed., *Continuity and Change: Aspects of Contemporary Norway.* New York: Oxford University Press, 1993. A collection of excellent essays by noted scholars on all aspects of contemporary life in Norway.

Barbara Øvstedal, *Norway.* New York: Hastings House, n.d. A combination of memoir, history, and travel guide, this volume contains useful, although somewhat dated information.

Sigmund Skard, *Classical Tradition in Norway.* Oslo: Universitetsforlaget, 1980. Scholarly work about the influence of antiquity on Norwegian art.

Erling Storusten, *Hurtigruten: The World's Most Beautiful Sea Voyage.* Narvik, Norway: Ofotens, 1999. Published as a companion for travelers on the Hurtigruten line, this volume contains a wide range of useful information about Norwegian geology, geography, history, and the lives of Norwegians today.

Elizabeth Su-Dale, *Culture Shock: Norway.* Portland, OR: Graphic Arts Center Publishing Co., 1995. One in a series, this volume explains customs and etiquette in Norway and provides a great deal of information about laws, lifestyles, culture, and daily activities.

Sigrid Undset, *Kristin Lavransdatter.* Translated by Tina Nunnally. New York: Penguin, 1997. A classic of Norwegian literature, this trilogy traces the life of a woman in medieval Norway who defies her parents to find her own happiness.

WEB SITES

CIA World Factbook. (www.cia.gov/cia/publications/factbook/no/html). Regularly updated statistical information about Norwegian economy and government, as well as information about the population.

Norway. (www.norway.org). Excellent range of information, but much of the site is in Norwegian.

INDEX

acid rain, 102
A Doll's House (Ibsen), 81
agriculture, 6
  Battle-Ax people and, 31
  government supports for,
    8–9, 59, 96
  in heartland, 27
  ironmaking, influence on,
    33
  lack of land suited for, 6
  rock drawings
    history of, 30
  short growing season and,
    22
  in southern regions, 25
  Vikings and, 38, 40
Aker, Brygge, 28
Akershus castle, 28, 46
aktiv, 64–65
alcohol, 75
Alvsson, Knut, 46
Amundsen, Roald, 17
animals
  lemmings, 18
  puffins, 100
  reindeer, 21, 100–101, 103
  whales, 23
architecture, 14, 88
Arctic, 22–25
Arctic Cathedral, 23
art
  in communities, 17
  government support of, 86
  painting, 84, 86
  pewterware, 79
  during Romantic Era, 52
  sculpture, 29, 86
  woodpainting , 25
As, Nils, 86
Asen, Ivar, 94
"At Akershus" (Ibsen), 46

athletics, 29
aurora borealis, 24

Baalsrud, Jan, 56
Backer, Harriet, 84
bandy (game), 63
Barents Sea, 6, 15, 26
Battle-Ax, 31
Begnadalen (valley), 26
Berg, Bøge, 86
Bergen (city), 6, 17, 19
  bubonic plague and, 43
  climate in, 19
  uprising in, 46
Bergen International Music
  Festival, 19
Betrayed (Skran), 83
Bjørnson, Bjørnstjerne, 80
Black Death, the, 43
Bloodax, Eirik, 40
Bluetooth, Harald, 40–41
Boat-Ax, 31
Bodø (town), 22, 24
Bøge, Kari, 84
Boine, Mari, 89, 90
bokmål (language), 9, 94
Borgund (town), 27
Bruin, Christopher, 52
Brundtland, Gro Harlem, 102
  as first woman prime minis-
    ter, 58
Bryggen, 19
Bull, Ole, 89
bunad (traditional costume),
  52
Bygdøy (island), 28–29

Canute, 41–42
Catholicism, 27, 47
Chancellor, Richard, 24–25
Charles the Bald (France), 35

Chernobyl
  effects of
    on environment, 100
    on reindeer population, 21
Christian III, 48
Christian IV, 47
Christianity
  Protestantism established
    in, 47, 48
  Sami and, 21
  Vikings and, 41
Christian of Oldenburg, 46
climate
  Arctic Circle and, 22–25
  Gulf Stream, effect on, 26
  isolation of population be-
    cause of, 10
  outdoor activities, effect on,
    60–62
clothing, 52, 78–89
coastal communities, 16–17
Collett, Camilla, 83
communism, 53
Copenhagen (Denmark), 49
culture
  art and, 28
  autonomy of, 50
  decline of native, 47
  differences in, 71
  of individualism, 10
  rock paintings and, 31
  Romantic Era and, 52
Culture Shock: Norway (Su-
  Dale), 94

Dag (Viking chieftain), 32
Dahl, J. C., 84
Dass, Petter, 80
Denmark, 7, 40–41, 46–47,
  104
Den Norske Tuistforeningen
  (DTN), 51
disease
  bubonic plague, 43
  in concentration camps, 57
  during Viking Era, 36
District Governor's Daughters,
  The (Collett), 83
Domaldi (Viking chieftain),
  32

Domkirke (church building),
  28
Dovrefjell (national park), 27
drugs, 75

economy
  autonomy of, 50
  depression and, 53
  future of, 92
  global outlook on, 104
  high taxes and, 11, 46, 95–98
  isolationism and, 103
  merchant class and, 40
  public works projects and,
    53
  shipping and, 28
  trade and, 38, 47
  during Viking Era, 36
  World War II, 55
education
  adult classes, 70
  equality in, 11–12, 66
  falling revenues, effect on,
    97
  government programs for,
    59
  literacy improved during
    Danish era, 47
  in northern cities, 59
  parent involvement in, 68
  religion and, 69
  Romantic Era, expansion
    during, 52
  secondary grades of, 66
  universities, 69–70
Eirik Bloodax, 40
Ekelund, Arn, 86
employment
  in Arctic region, 22
  fishing as, 92
environment
  economy and, 100
  leading roll in protecting,
    58, 59, 103
  management of resources
    and, 12, 101–103
  stresses on, 92
Erickson, Harald Greycloak,
  40

Eriksson, Leif, 36
Ericksson, Magnus, 44
Erik of Pomerania, 45
Erik the Red, 36
ethnic minorities, 98–99
European Union, 58
  opposition to joining, 59,
    103–104

family, 9
  children and, 73–75
  men and, 75
Fehn, Sverre, 88, 89
feriepenger (holiday pay), 72
Finnmark, 24
fishing
  in Arctic region, 23
  ecosystem changes and, 24
  the future of, 92
  life centered around, 17
Fjolnir (Viking chieftain), 32
fjords, 6, 15
Fløibanen (cable car), 19
folk culture, 87, 89
food, 74
foreign relations, 12, 50, 92
  support of world nations, 59
forestry, 23, 101–102
Forkbeard, Svein, 41
"400 Year Sleep, The" (Carter),
    48
France, 49
  Viking sack of Paris, 35
Frederik, Christian, 49
Frey (Viking god), 39
Frognerparken, 29

Gaardner, Jostein, 84
Galdhopiggen (mountain),
    27
Gate, Karl Johan's, 28, 50
Geiranger hang, 14
geography, 13–30
  aurora borealis and, 24
  Arctic Circle and, 22, 24
  effect on ruling nations, 47
  fjords and, 15
  general facts about, 6
  midnight sun and, 24
  national character forged by, 8

giants, 87
Gjende (lake), 27
glassware, 79
Glittertinden (mountain), 27
Godwinson, Harold, 42
Gokstad ship, 34
government
  of chieftains, 32
  constitutional monarchy es-
    tablished, 51–52
  lagting and, 38
  legal system and, 37
  local councils established,
    50
  popular assemblies in, 38
  socialism, 59
  social programs and, 11–12
  Storting, 50, 51
Great Britain, 57, 42
  mining Norwegian harbors
    and, 55
Greenland, 26, 36
Grieg, Edvard, 52, 89
Grini, 54

Hadrada, Harald, 40
Hafrsfjord, Battle of, 18
Håkon, 44
Håkon IV, 42
Håkon VII, 51
Halfdan the Black, 33
halling (folkdance), 89
Hallingdalen (valley), 26
Hamar (town), 27
Hamar Olympic Hall, 88
Hammerfest (town), 23–24
Hamsun, Knut, 83
Hanseatic League, 46
Harald V, 11
Haraldsson, Saint Olav, 20,
    41–42
Hardanger fiddle, 89
Hardanger plateau, 26
Hardangervidda (plateau),
    26
Hardråda, Harald (Harald the
    Hard), 42
Hårfagri, Harald, 18, 38, 41
Hastings, Battle of, 42
Haugeland, Arnold, 86

Hebrides Islands, 36
Hedda Gabler (play), 82
Heddal (town), 25
Heimskringla (Sturluson), 80
Henie, Sonja, 64
hiking, 63
Hitler, Adolf, 54, 83
Hoel, Sigrid, 83
Holberg, Ludvig, 80
Holmenkollen ski jump, 29,
  64–65
Home of the Giants, 26
housing, 73–74
  decoration of, 13, 77–78
  summer cottages, 17
human rights, 59
Hunger (Hamsun), 83
Hurtigruten coastal steamer,
  6, 17
hytter (mountain cabins), 29,
  60–16

Ibsen, Henrik, 46, 80–82
ice hockey, 63
Iceland, 39, 40
idrett (strenuous sports),
  63–66
immigration, 12
  effect on social structure,
    98–99
international relations, 12
Ireland, 35
iron, 22–23
  effect on economy, 32–33
  World War II, factor in, 56
islands, 6, 15

Jante Law, 11
Jotunheimen, 26–27

Kalmar (Sweden), 45
Kalmar Union, 46
Karl XIV Johan, 50
  See also Gate, Karl Johan's
Karvik (town), 22
Kielland, Kitty, 84
Kirkenes, 6, 17, 23, 26
Kleiva, Per, 86
klippfisk (cod), 24
Knivskjellodden (promon-

tory), 24
Køltzow, Live, 84
Kon Tiki (museum), 29
Kristin Lavransdatter (Undset),
  83
Krohg, Christian, 84
Krohg, Osa, 84

labor laws, 72–73
  unions and, 51, 52
  unrest and, 53
Labor Party, 52, 59
Lady King, 55
lagting (second assembly), 38
language
  bokmål, 9
  decline of original Norwe-
    gian, 47
  language of instruction dur-
    ing Danish era, 48
  nationally recognized, 94
  new written, 52
  nynorsk, 9
Lapps, 21
  see also Sami
lays (narrative poems), 39
lemmings, 18
Liberal Party, 102
Lie-Jørgensen, Thorbjørn, 86
Lillehammer
  glassware production in, 79
  Olympic Games in, 21, 27, 88
Lindesfarne, 35
literature
  contemporary women's is-
    sues in, 84
  female authors, 83
  Golden Age of, 80
Lofoten Islands, 15, 47
Loki (Viking god), 39
Lord Nelson, 49
Løveid, Cecilie, 83
Lutheran church, 69
  see also Christianity

Magnus the Lawmender,
  42–43
Margareta, 44
midnight sun, 22, 24
Minister President, 8, 54

Ministry of Church and Education, 65
Mjøsa (lake), 27
Munch, Edvard, 84–85
museums, 27, 29
music, 88–91
Mussolini, Benito, 54
mythology
  gods of, 39
  in literature, 80
  Pietism and, 48
  pride in, 52

Napoleon, 49
National Gallery, 28, 84
National Theater, 28
National Unification Party, 54
NATO (North Atlantic Treaty Organization), 59, 103
natural resources, 59
  in Arctic region, 22
  exploited by ruling neighbors, 47
  future of, 92
  in the heartland, 28
  minerals, 8
Nazi, 8
  concentration camps in Norway, 54
  influence on Norwegian independence, 104
  leaders in Norway, 57
  occupation and bombing by, 17, 55–57
  Vidkun Quisling and, 54
Newfoundland, 36
Negri, Francesco, 25
Nerdrum, Odd, 86
Nesch, Rolf, 86
New World, 7, 36
Nidaros, 20
Nidaros Cathedral, 20
Nid (river), 20
Nordmarka, 29
Norges Idrellsforbund (NIF), 65
Norheim, Sondre, 64
Norsk Folkemuseum, 29
Nordkapp (North Cape), 24

northern lights. *See* aurora borealis
Norway
  Denmark and Sweden, relations with, 7, 46, 49
  first battle of united, 42
  independence desire for, 7, 10–11, 40–41
  individualism in, 103–104
  World War II and, 54–57
Norway: The Rough Guide (Brown and Lee), 18, 31, 39, 84
Norwegian Independence Day, 49–50
Norwegian National Council, 47
Norwegians
  activities of, 60–65
  desire for privacy, 9, 10, 71
  patriotism and, 59
Norwegian Sea, 15, 101
Numendalen, 26
Nygaardsvold, Johan, 53, 55
nynorsk (language), 9, 52, 94

Odin (Viking god), 39
oil and natural gas, 11
  in the Arctic Circle, 22
  effect on social programs, 97
  future of, 92
  standard of living and, 12
Olav V, 65
Olav, Saint. *See* Haraldsson Saint Olav
Olay, 41
Olympic Games
  in Lillehammer, 27, 88
  medals from, 65
  Sami in, 21
Orkney Islands, 47
Oskar I, 50
Oslo, 20, 28–29,
  national capital, 25
  renamed as Christiania, 48
  uprising in, 46
  weekend activities in, 75–76
Oslofjord (fjord), 15
Our Common Future (UN report), 58

Peer Gynt (Ibsen), 89
Peer Gynt Suite (Grieg), 89
Period of Greatness, 42
pewter, 79
Pietism, 14, 48
Poetic Edda (mythological poems), 39
puffins, 100

quisling (traitor), 8
Quisling, Vidkun, 8, 54

Raknerud, Gladys Nilssen, 86
Red Maiden, 35
religion
  education and, 69
  Pietism, 14, 48
  Protestantism, 41, 47–48
Rjukan, 57
Romantic Era, 52
Rondane (national park), 27
Røros (mining town), 28
rosemaling (wood painting), 25, 78
russ (secondary school graduate), 67
Russia, 6, 53
Russian Revolution, 21

Sami, 21
  Olympic Games and, 21
  Christianity, conversion to, 48
  culture, preservation of, 21
  reindeer and, 100–101, 103
  required study of, 68
Sandel, Cora, 83
Sandemose, Aksel, 11
Sandvig, Anders, 27
Scandinavia, 7, 26, 44
Scandinavian welfare model, 93
Scream, The (Munch), 84
Shetland Bus, 7
Shetland Islands, 36, 47
Sigurdsson, Håkon, 41
Sinnetagen (Vigeland), 86
skiing, 6
  birthplace of, 25
  invented by, 64

major winter pastime, 60–63
Skran, Amalie, 83
slavery, 40
soccer, 63
Socialist Party, 102
social programs
  health care and, 59
  management of natural resources and, 12
  political and economic philosophy and, 59
  quality of life and, 11
  reforms and, 52
  taxes and, 11, 95–98
  welfare state and , 93–95
Sophie's World (Gaardner), 84
Soviet Union, 8, 65
sports
  activities, 63, 65
  quality of life and, 92
  social life and, 62–63
  Vikings and, 29
Stavanger (city), 17, 18
Stavanger Cathedral, 18
stave church, 14, 25, 27,88
Stiklestad, Battle of, 42
Storting, 50, 51, 102
Sturluson, Snorri, 80
Sug (Løveid), 84
Sweden
  alliance with, 7
  Norway, controlled by, 41, 49, 104

taxes
  rural communities and, 9
  uprising against foreign, 46
Telemark region, 25
Telemark turn, 64
Terboven, Josef, 57
Thjodolf, 32
Thor (Viking god), 39
ting, 38
torget (marketplace), 19
transportation, 6
  commuting, 71
  difficulty with, 6
  the future and, 12
  network of tunnels and bridges, 8

public works projects and, 53
railroads, 23, 26
Treaty of Kiel, 49
Trollfjord (fjord), 15
trolls, 87
Tromsø (town), 22, 23
Trondheim (city), 6, 17, 19–20
Trondheimfjord, 15
Tronds, 41
Tryggvason, Olav, 41
tur (tour), 76

Undset, Sigrid, 83
United Nations, 58, 59
University of Oslo, 50, 69

Valhalla, 39
Valkyries, 39
Vampire, The (Munch), 84
Vesteralen Island, 15
Vigeland, Gustav, 29, 86
Vigelandsparken, 29, 86
Viking museum, 29
Vikings, 6, 18
  architecture, influence on, 14
  art, influence on, 77
  development of merchant class and, 40
  discovery of the New World by, 36
  end of conquest by, 42
  government and, 38–39
  legends about, 31
  in literature, 80

religion, 41
war and, 35, 37, 40
written language and, 32
Vinland Sagas, 36
Von Westen, Thomas, 48

Waitz, Grete, 64
Wales, 37
water sports, 63
We Die Alone (Howarth), 56
Weidemann, Jakob, 86
wergild (Viking law), 37
William the Conqueror, 42
Winge, Sigrud, 86
Woden (Viking god), 39
women
  as authors, 83
  feminism and, 81
  in literature, 83–84
  in politics, 58, 102
  rights of, 52
World Health Organization, 58
World War I
  neutrality declared during, 52
  Norwegian casualties during, 53
World War II
  German occupation of Norway during, 8, 17, 23
  resistance during, 8, 56–57

Ynglinga Tal (Tjodolf), 32
yoik (song), 21
Youth and Idrett, 65

Picture Credits

Cover Photo: © B. & C. Alexander/Photo Researchers
© Bettmann/Corbis, 82, 83
© Corbis, 54
Laurel Corona, 22, 36, 61, 78, 86, 87
Destination Stryn & Nordfjord, 62
Fjord Norge, 63, 79
Fjord Norge/Knut Bry, 17
Fjord Norge/ Per Nybø, 19
Fjord Norge/Hanne Sundbø, 10
Hulton Getty/Archive Photos, 41, 50, 51
Eric Lessing/Art Resource, NY, 85
North Wind Picture Archives, 39
© Notra/Knut Bry/Norwegian Tourist Board, 73
Norwegian Tourist Board, 9, 20, 21, 25, 27, 88, 89
Norwegian Tourist Board/Nancy Bundt, 13, 65
Photodisc, 100
© Reuters Newmedia Inc./Corbis, 58
© Paul A. Souders/Corbis, 68, 96
Scala/Art Resource, NY, 84
Martha Schierholz, 7, 16, 34, 55
© S jostedt, Ulf/FPG International, 33
© Stock Montage, 45
© Winnifred Wisniewski; Frank Lane Picture Agency/
    Corbis, 12

About the Author

Laurel Corona lives in Lake Arrowhead, California, and teaches English and Humanities at San Diego City College. She has a Master's degree from the University of Chicago and a Ph.D. from the University of California at Davis.